The Vanishing Root

The Vanishing Root
Eddie McCaffrey's Story

by

Maurus Green O.S.B.

New City

London   Dublin   Edinburgh

First published in 1994

by

New City
57 Twyford Avenue
London W3 9PZ

**A CIP catalogue record for this book is available from the
British Library**

ISBN 0 904287 50 5

Typeset by Phoenix Typesetting, Ilkley, West Yorkshire

Printed and Bound by
The Cromwell Press, Broughton Gifford, Wiltshire

CONTENTS

Foreword – The Problem: A Letter to
the Editor 7

1 In his Liverpool Home 9

2 Dublin 19

3 Wheelchair Blessings 25

4 Mary's Answer 31

5 City on a Hill 43

6 A Job at Last 51

7 As I Have Loved You 59

8 New Generation 65

9 The Vanishing Root 73

10 The Race towards God 95

11 Mary, I Come Running to You 115

Epitaph 123

FOREWORD

The Problem: A Letter to the Editor

Dear Callan,

You have asked me to tell the story of Eddie McCaffrey, perhaps because I knew him longer even than his closest friends.

How do you write about someone to whom nothing seemed to happen? A person without even an obedient left foot he could train to type, or teeth for writing and painting like the man with no arms or legs. Lifeless muscles simply forbid all activity, even the most elementary.

Yet you yourself have written, 'He was like an atomic reactor, in the midst of which he himself was being destroyed to produce a constant burst of energy, only this energy was all love for each individual he met.

'The last time I met him, at a concert in Dublin's National Stadium, he was in his wheelchair, fairly close to the front. Just before the start of the concert we managed to exchange a few words. I shall never forget them.

'I asked him how he was. He replied, "Fine. I lose strength every day, but who needs strength?"

'That last comment was said with a mixture of humour and total sincerity. He could hardly lift his head and barely move his hands, but I realized he meant precisely what he said. He was completely at ease with his situation, detached from it, so that he could talk quite dispassionately about what was happening to him. Yet, at the same time, he saw the whole thing from a divine point of view. He felt that what mattered was not his strength or power or activity but to be one with Jesus on the cross, in perfect harmony with his cry to the Father, "Why have you forsaken me?"

'We did not say much more. What had been said was quite enough. Although it was communication with words, what was said also went far beyond what could be spoken.'

For nearly two years I have mulled over the task you have set me, quite unable to see what that task was. Not only did Eddie do nothing, he left no diary to reveal his inner life, and even the hundreds of letters he managed to scrawl with grim determination have vanished – just a few pearls remain.

Only now, after analysing your vision of that 'atomic reactor of love', do I begin to see light. What you are asking is this: how did Eddie become that reactor in which he himself was being destroyed to produce that constant burst of energy?

For Eddie was not always like that. Behind those words 'I lose strength every day, but who needs strength?' lie years of frustration, disappointment and struggle.

At that concert, Callan, you met the victorious Eddie, the gentle, humorous conqueror of himself, plagued by his familiar enemy turned friend, that disease which kills by inches, muscular dystrophy.

This book must make that struggle real or be rejected by you, its editor.

Maurus Green, O.S.B.   June 1991.

1

In his Liverpool Home

I first met Edward McCaffrey when he was nine or ten. He had already come face to face with tragedy. His parents had married during the war and lived in our Benedictine parish of St. Austin's, Grassendale, South Liverpool. Jack, his father, had served in the Army, surviving the evacuation of Dunkirk and the crossing of the Rhine.

Edward was born on 16 March 1949. Two years later Jack was killed in an accident outside our church in the Aigburth Road. His mother, Margaret, was shattered. Her world had collapsed. Her long dream of settling down to family life on her husband's release from the Forces had only just been fulfilled in the birth of their beautiful child. Now Edward would never know his Dad. What strange fate had brought him safely through the long war, only to be killed on his own doorstep?

There was little time to grieve. Eddie was missing his father's loving presence and had to be consoled with the assurance that he had gone to heaven, a fact he accepted with the simplicity of a child. Somehow Margaret had to shield him from her own sorrow, determined to keep his life as happy and balanced as possible. Fortunately he was a cheerful child with a strong sense of humour.

To support them both, Margaret was able to take over

her husband's job as Insurance Agent. This meant putting Eddie in a local Nursery School, since her aged parents, who lived nearby, could not cope with a small child. There he stayed happily with the other children until he was five years old, when Margaret moved him to our Junior School at St. Austin's.

When he was three or four, Margaret became aware that something was wrong with his legs. He was running slower than normal and he had a cumbersome way of climbing stairs. The hospital noted the tightness of his Achilles' tendons and prescribed physiotherapy to loosen them. Eddie happily accepted this treatment and no one paid particular attention to his growing awkwardness.

At school, he joined in everything, especially games. He was crazy about football, but his lack of speed meant he always had to play in goal. By the time he was seven, Margaret became worried that he was falling about so much in the playground. Each time he had to crawl on hands and knees to the nearest wall before he could clamber to his feet.

By now Margaret had remarried. Eddie had introduced her to 'Uncle John' whom he often met in a small friend's home down the road. John Neylon had come from the West of Ireland for work in the building trade. After their marriage, he became the ideal stepfather and brought great happiness into the home.

Shortly after their marriage, work moved the family to Durham where Eddie attended an old-fashioned school with a huge fire and guard to warm the single classroom during that cold winter. He and Margaret enjoyed the walk to school, climbing the ice-covered road and skidding down the slopes through the snow. She was relieved, however, when work took them back to Liverpool and she could care for her elderly parents once more.

There, it became clear that Eddie must see a specialist, since the physiotherapy was having no effect. His condition was simply deteriorating. The specialist diagnosed Muscular Dystrophy, a disease Margaret had never heard of. When she asked what the treatment was, he replied to her horror, 'There isn't any. It will get progressively worse and you can't expect him to live out his teens.'

His parents were completely devastated. Overnight their world had turned upside-down. How could they hide their anguish and prevent it disrupting their serene family life? Eddie must continue to feel relaxed and happy at home. He was too young to be told this news which he could not have begun to understand. Now they had to sustain each other and carry on as if nothing unusual had happened.

Yet Margaret's suffering and confusion were too intimate to be fully shared with John, as she searched desperately for someone to turn to, someone who could understand her from within and give her support. Even her old friend, Josie Grue, who was proving such a rock of comfort, could not do that.

Margaret had been a Catholic all her life, attending Mass and receiving the sacraments, but she had never experienced a deep personal relationship with Jesus and Mary. In her desperation, she turned to Mary and somehow found her, no longer as Queen of Heaven, remote and beautiful in glory, but as a personal friend, a mother like herself with whom she could chat, 'Mary, you suffered so much because of your beloved only Son. You were told a sword would pierce your heart because of him, so you understand how I feel now. Help me to have your courage and serenity, so that Eddie's childhood is not marred by my worry and anxiety.'

After conversations like this, she always felt that Mary was supporting her, bringing peace into her heart, so that she was able to live each day, playing and laughing with him, making his childhood as carefree as possible.

Eddie was well aware of his difficulty with running and even walking quickly, but he knew nothing of the doctor's forecast. He accepted his condition and was absorbed by football. Sports were his ruling passion. Sometimes he would be taken to sports stadiums, but mostly he saw games on television. He knew every player by name and spent hours filling scrapbooks with their photos. Naturally, Everton and Liverpool were his favourite teams. Every night he prayed, 'Please God make my legs better, so I can be a footballer.'

Eddie was no angel. He was popular with the other boys at school, but that did not stop them jeering at him for his slowness and laughing at him when he fell down for no apparent reason. 'If only I could run and catch them, I'd give them a good thump,' he confided to his Mother. His class would have the occasional sports afternoon, and he would have been so thrilled to have brought home a medal, but he began to realize this was a dream that would never come true. He was very downhearted and said, 'Mum, do you mind having a boy like me?' His mother told him that when God was creating him, he knew exactly how he would be and had searched the earth to find the exact mother for him. He had given them to each other. So no other boy would make her happy, and no other mother would be right for him. This explanation really pleased him, and Margaret thanked Mary in her heart for answering her prayer to give her the right words when Eddie needed reassurance.

Eventually, it became clear that Eddie could not cope with the rough and tumble of an ordinary junior school and he transferred to one for handicapped children. He settled down quite happily in this Special School with its caring teachers and excellent chalet-type buildings in the grounds of a large house. He was a good mixer and made friends easily. In fact, he noticed that most of the other handicapped children were much worse off physically then himself, although this was not always true. Besides, living at home enabled him to keep in touch with his old friends from St. Austin's.

About this time, Eddie's parents took him to Lourdes to ask for Mary's help. He thoroughly enjoyed the trip, though not in any religious sense. He was simply thrilled with his first experience of flying, staying in a hotel and mixing with so many 'strange' people. And, of course, Lourdes was the home of many famous rugby players which made it doubly interesting. He went to the baths each day. He found this a bit of an ordeal, but he was very attracted to the large fatherly French priest who took charge of him after his mother had undressed him. Coming out into the warm sunshine after his first bath, his mother asked him if he had asked Mary to cure him, as she had been doing. He looked up at her and replied, 'Oh no, I just asked her to keep me a good boy always.' Margaret realized that Mary was Eddie's mother too and had her own way of speaking to him.

One afternoon, Margaret and John were enjoying a cup of coffee in the lounge of the hotel, and, as Eddie walked with great difficulty, they thought he was nearby. They were very startled when the manager approached them and asked if they could kindly control their child. They were amazed. Apparently, Eddie had discovered the lift and was having great fun going up and down time and time again. It was a tiny lift, like a long bird-cage, and as people arrived at the floor they wanted, Eddie would shoot out his finger and press them back to the ground floor again. It was superb fun – the people all shouting at him in many foreign tongues and Ed howling with laughter. It was an embarrassing moment, but after John and Margaret explained to him that he couldn't do that again, he never did, although he often looked longingly at the lift.

A single-decker school bus used to collect Eddie from near his home, the attendant helping Margaret to get him on and off. This worked well so long as he was able to walk. The trouble began when he was ten and could no longer walk. He had to take to a wheelchair which was too wide for the narrow coach door. He was also too big and heavy for Margaret to lift on to the bus. So he had to leave the Special School and make do with a home teacher, Miss Birchall, who used to come twice a week for two-hourly sessions. Though she became a good friend of Margaret and Eddie, he was being deprived of the social life of the classroom. Margaret felt strongly that contact with other children was part of the education he needed.

Just then, a senior school for handicapped children had been built at Sandfield Park, about five miles away. This beautiful school was opened by Douglas Bader, the legless pilot. The snag was that there was no transport, and pupils had to make their own way to the school.

Margaret went down to the Education Committee to remedy this situation. She asked to see the Manager, but was told he was out. All day long she waited. Each time she asked to see him, she was put off with a different excuse. Somehow she knew he was still in the building. She continued to wait. She saw all the clerical staff go home and the cleaners arrive. Still she waited. Eventually the manager had to emerge to make his way home. Margaret collared him. She pointed out that all parents had the right to send their children to the school of their choice. Because of her son's handicap, she had decided to send him to the Sandfield Park School. She demanded to know what was the point of such a school if a child could not walk to get there.

She explained that, although the family had a minibus with a ramp for a wheelchair, Eddie's father had to go to work early and he was too heavy for Margaret to lift into the bus alone. The manager had to capitulate and arranged for a lady who delivered school dinners to take Eddie plus wheelchair to and from school, getting help at either end with lifting him. This worked well until the Education Committee objected to paying for the extra petrol and increased salary of the dinner lady.

To her delighted astonishment, Margaret was rescued at this point by a very irate mother of another handicapped child. This mother descended on the Education Committee and refused to be put off by the staff. Believing in direct confrontation, she simply marched in on the manager and bashed him over the head with her handbag!

That did the trick. In no time at all the Education Committee produced a van specially equipped for wheelchairs with hydraulic lift and clamps to fasten them to the van floor. So the van, complete with driver and attendant, used to call each morning and evening to pick Eddie up for the double journey. From the start he loved the school with its excellent teachers, specially trained to teach handicapped children.

When Eddie was about twelve, he was plunged into crisis by his mother having to go into hospital for complicated treatment. She was away for two-and-a-half months, after which she had to have radium treatment, so that it was an agonizing length of time before she was fit enough to care for Eddie again. All this meant that Eddie had to move into a residential school for the handicapped for two whole terms. Just as he was beginning to wonder whether he had lost his mother altogether, his grandfather, to whom he was very close, died suddenly. His world was falling apart.

So it was a question of John, his stepfather, to the rescue. He was an ingenious man and discovered a way to see Eddie beyond the strict visiting hours for parents. Eddie was delighted to find him arriving also every Sunday morning and taking him and the other Catholic children to Mass. This he followed up with a run-out in his van with ice-creams all round. It became so popular that the non-Catholic children wanted the same treatment. So, having done his duty by the Catholics, John would return and do the same for them. When work got in the way, two of John's friends obligingly took over from him. These church outings became an established thing and continued long after Eddie had left.

Back at home, it took Eddie some time to conquer his fear of losing his mother. In fact, they were both having their first mutual taste of the fragility of their former harmony. Margaret was still weak and exhausted after her long illness, whereas her son needed constant reassurance that she would not suddenly vanish. Even his growing love of football was challenged by the presence of his grandmother. She was disgusted by his monopoly of the television sports coverage. She had no time for Westerns either. Inevitably there were clashes between this eighty year old lady and her thirteen year old grandson, bubbling over with frustrated energy, confined to his wheelchair and shod in his football boots. But, although Margaret often had to restore peace, they came to value and appreciate one another as time went by.

Sandfield Park marked a turning point for Eddie in an unexpected way. One of his teachers specialized in Current Affairs. He had a flair for involving his pupils in fascinating discussions in which Eddie became the leader.

This was undoubtedly due to John Neylon, one of the best informed and most articulate of parents. John opened up his horizons on the world affairs discussed at school, so that he would return to class greatly enriched with a more mature grasp of his own opinions. For the first time in his life he excelled among his equals as a respected source of information and enlightenment made acceptable by his humorous quips. This boost to his morale coincided with his growing sense of social justice which became acute by the time he was sixteen, the age for leaving Sandfield Park. Just then his grandmother died leaving the family free to move house if they so wished.

2

Dublin

John Neylon had never really felt at home in England. His heart always harked back to his homeland, to his ideal, a farmhouse in Co. Clare, open to all. He wanted his home to be like that, where hospitality made all comers feel welcome. Despite its renowned friendliness, a large industrial city like Liverpool frustrated all his efforts.

Deep within John, too, lurked a passionate love of Ireland as the object of centuries of injustice, a cause he would champion with some heat in discussion. A sympathetic audience was more readily available back home.

Now that he was free of all ties, he seized his opportunity. Not that Ireland itself was entirely new to Margaret and Eddie. They had spent many happy holidays over there with John at the wheel and Eddie as navigator. He had soon learnt to steer them clear of the seaside where the sand would clog the wheels of his chair and make progress impossible.

Latterly too, they had come to Dublin for regular injections from a specialist who claimed to have found some cure for muscular dystrophy. This turned out to be a cruel deception after a couple of years, despite Eddie's initial conviction that his arms were getting stronger. Once more Margaret had to mask her pain and wait until he reached the conclusion that the treatment was doing him no good. Yet another proof that his disease was progressive and relentless.

But Dublin as a permanent home was another matter. No new home in sight. No Liverpool or familiar friends for Margaret. No school, no friends, no football for Eddie. Just a gloomy farmhouse belonging to John's parents on the outskirts of Dublin, with a yard hardly designed for wheelchairs. They felt trapped without their old van which had come to the end of its days. Another van was out of the question until they had paid for the new home for which John was searching.

Of this period Eddie wrote:

'The first six months there were a time of terrible suffering and frustration. We were living with my grandmother and while my step-father was out at work, my mother and I used to spend the long days together in the house. I was unable to get out and this impressed upon me the fact of my disability!'

His dream of going to University had also to be postponed until he had enough subjects to pass Matriculation. These he would first have to obtain in the Leaving Certificate. Eddie had set his heart on University as a last resort, convinced that his handicap did not make him any less able than other people. In any case, he must qualify for some career, if only to give meaning to his existence.

To prepare him to pass in the required subjects, a teacher was found to tutor him twice a week. This new friend was willing to travel the extra ten miles to the house John eventually decided to buy for the family.

This was No. 40 Lower Dodder Road in the rather rural area of Rathfarnham, South Dublin. As a home, it was a luxury for Eddie. He had never lived in a bungalow before where his chair had access to all rooms. No stairs to get in the way. He had only to press a button to steer where he wanted.

But the house, set in a single row, was still the limit of his world. Across the road flowed the narrow river Dodder, its surface occasionally graced by majestic swans, but more often troubled by gulls diving for minnows. Through the line of trees on the opposite bank peeped a single redbrick house which caught his imagination.

Just then, his tutor was introducing him to English Literature. Eddie was fascinated by his insights into the major prose writers, playwrights and poets. It was now that he was moved to try his hand at poetry, and with some success. An early example is the impact of the redbrick house upon his inner torment:

> Redbrick house on riverbank,
> Looking down at me from opposite bank
> Through a mask of greenery.
> In what way do you see me?
> Like you I hide behind a mask,
> A mask that nature endows
> And whose powers I use
> To neglect my fellow man
> Whom I see through the masked haze.
> Their full life I forever chase
> But I lose and hate their pace.
> Unlike Redbrick house on riverbank
> I accept the sun that reflects
> On the waters along riverbank.
> But, when the wind ripples the trout stream
> And sends dark clouds above me,
> I retreat to the care and to the sympathy
> Nature's mask provides for me.
> I want to be free as the elements

But I refuse the involved responsibility
Beyond the barrier's refuge created by nature.
And so a cognitional coward, among
      incognitional cowards,
Plays humanity's benevolent game,
Till reality and pain
Replace the benevolent prize.
Then cowardice is realized.

This vivid picture of the view through his window must have recalled to Margaret those poignant moments when she caught Eddie's look of pain, as he watched passing groups of boys, off to play football or other games in the neighbouring park. She knew he longed to join them.

More worrying to her was his determination to go to University, an impossible dream which she felt was doomed from the start. Even if he should succeed in matriculating, his difficulties would be insurmountable. He would need constant help with his basic needs, never mind moving up and down steps and from place to place. Yet she dare not voice her fears. She could not deprive him of all hope.

About a year after they had settled in Dublin, came the moment of truth. Eddie had to take the Leaving Certificate in the three subjects he had been cramming with his tutor, English, History and Geography. Margaret's anguish was intensified as she saw John depart with him to a strange school to join the examinees. She knew he was dreading it and prayed for him all that day.

Sure enough he was the object of keen interest among the other boys. A boy in a wheelchair was a novelty. He felt completely out of place, especially as John had to leave him at the school early to get to work. This ordeal lasted for three days. Each day he was wheeled to his desk and for three hours he did his best to answer the questions. He would arrive home completely exhausted.

Anxiously, they awaited the results. Surely, Margaret felt, all the hours he had spent studying in his room day after day must now be rewarded. Alas, it was not to be. He had passed in all three subjects but his grades were below the standard required for matriculation. As he remarked later,

'That goal had meant so much to me. No matter how hard I tried to be equal, I felt inferior. Although I knew I could not be equal to other people physically, I had hoped at least to get a good education. Now this hope had collapsed. So I decided that work was the answer!

'After a lot of fruitless searching, I started a three month management course for handicapped people. This was a bitter experience. I used to travel to the centre where the course was held, by taxi. Sometimes the taximen refused to help me out of the taxi because they said I was too heavy to lift, while others would be very obliging. But I would hear the next day that the driver had refused to come for me. In the end I had to phone to say that I would not be able to complete the course.'

3

Wheelchair Blessings

On all fronts, failure stared him full in the face. He would never now be a footballer, never get to University, never find a career. 'Stop the World,' he would say, 'I want to get on.'

At this juncture, Eddie was rescued by the Dublin Wheelchair Association. A lady called at the house to invite him to sample its weekly meetings at Clontarf. He agreed to give it a try. To meet other wheelchair victims would be a fresh experience. So a new world, which included holidays and social gatherings, opened up to him.

He became a close friend of Paddy, a muscular dystrophy man like himself, a singer and musician who excelled at the guitar. Paddy inspired Eddie's own love of music and fired his desire to play. A guitar was bought for him, but he could not hold it for long. Any wind instrument was out because his muscles were too weak to hold it to his mouth. Faced with yet another failure, Eddie had to content himself with hours of record playing. He loved all music, whether modern or classical. He even fancied he had a voice. Listening to his efforts, his parents had to confess that this was not one of the gifts God had bestowed on their son.

One of the delights of the Wheelchair Association was the regular outings to the major football and hurling matches at Croke Park, Dublin's Wembley. Wheelchair patients were welcomed free of charge. They sat in rows along the touch-line, absorbed by the skills of their favourite teams. Cheering madly, they felt as though they were playing.

One day, when the Wheelchair Association Manager was away from Clontarf, news came through to Eddie and the others at the Association Centre that, in future, wheelchairs would not be allowed at the Croke Park finals. The members were so indignant they rang up the Evening Paper to voice their wrath. A reporter came out only to find himself confronted by furious men and women. He was delighted and took their fighting statement back to the office. This decision was not only grossly unfair in that it penalized a minority group, it was also unjust because it imposed a double handicap on an already disadvantaged group. Why had they been singled out? Now they could not support their teams which they had followed all the year, and at the moment their backing was most needed.

Next day their story was front page news. The Association Manager could not believe his eyes. Furious, he summoned the members into his office. He had wanted to keep the whole thing quiet. This public fuss could only damage the Association and even lead to loss of financial support. He fairly slated his members but they refused to give way. They insisted they had every right to speak up for themselves.

'Why should we keep quiet and not say anything just because we are handicapped?' He had no answer and the matter was dropped.

In an unexpected way, the Association benefited John Neylon. Indirectly, it brought about the fulfilment of his dream for his home to be open to all. As Eddie's circle of friends grew, so wheelchair patients began to gather, until wheelchair parties became the regular thing. John would find himself faced with ten or twelve guests in wheel-chairs for singsongs, discussions and general merriment, all drawn by a truly Irish welcome.

Paddy, whose handicap was not as advanced as Eddie's, was in charge of entertainment at the weekly Association social. He soon had Eddie acting as transport director. Being a Dubliner, born and bred, he knew many people whose names and addresses he passed on to Eddie who soon had them drawn up in two lists, one for people willing to give lifts and the other for those requiring lifts. So he would spend his mornings on the phone linking up the two, an occupation he thrived on.

Yet, while he made firm friends with the other men and women in the Association, Eddie felt there was an emptiness within him. He wanted normal friends to help him integrate the handicapped into ordinary society. He resented the general tendency to isolate the handicapped as though they were almost a different species. This, he felt, was a grave injustice.

So, when he heard that a youth club was about to start up in his parish, he decided to join. Perhaps here he would find the answer. To some extent he did, though at first he had to win over the non-handicapped youngsters who showed the usual awkwardness in the presence of a wheelchair and tended to steer clear of him.

He made special friends with Billy who solved Eddie's own transport problem. Once a week saw Billy pushing him to the club in his wheelchair.

Once the ice was broken, Eddie became the centre of attraction, both because of his genius for friendship and because of his handicap. As usual he shone in discussion. He always loved a good argument and his sense of fun was a brake upon heated discussion. Not always, however. He was not only a bit of a rebel but had a strong sense of right and wrong. He could be very firm if there was any shadow of injustice affecting his friends.

This, in fact, blew up after he had been made vice-president of the club, an honour that thrilled him. Unfortunately, the priest in charge had set ideas which he was trying to impose on the members. They had equally firm views as to how they wanted the club to function. Young adults, they refused to be dictated to. In the course of the heated argument that followed, they decided to walk out. In desperation, the priest turned to Eddie,

'Well, Eddie, you're not going to walk out on me, are you?'

With great dignity, Eddie replied, 'Well, unfortunately, Father, I'm not able to walk out, but my friend, Billy, will push me out.'

The priest would not give way, while the club members were equally stubborn. They decided to picket the club. For several weeks thereafter, the members walked up and down with Billy pushing Eddie in his wheelchair. Eventually everyone cooled down, but the club was never quite the same again.

It was not just the handicapped who were drawn to Eddie's home. Their relatives and friends started drifting in too. One of these, the beautiful sister of one of his friends, used to pop in often just to see how he was. She completely took his breath away and he fell deeply in love with her, but not she with him. This was an agony he kept bravely to himself. He never declared his love but the realization that it was not returned, plunged him into deep depression.

Perhaps nothing is quite so devastating as unrequited love. For Eddie it was worse because it not only crowned the collapse of his world in all departments, but deprived him of his two chief sources of consolation: Mass and the

Association. His love was hopeless and the hurt ravaged him deeply.

Margaret used to have to put him to bed, undressing him and helping him into bed with the aid of a lift. Often when she looked in to say 'goodnight', she would find him with tears streaming down his face and wetting his pillow. His arms, worn out with muscular fatigue, were unable to wipe them away. His emotional turmoil stared from his eyes. She was in confusion, uncertain what to do or say, her silence filled with pity beyond all telling. In the past, she had been like a background, helping him over his troubles in an unobtrusive way. Now she had no answers, no easy solutions, just her silent support.

Sunday Mass was a normal part of their family life. Now Eddie became so depressed that religion held no interest or consolation for him. He turned against everything. At Mass he had to be pushed to the front to find a space for his wheelchair. He commented:

'Everyone stares at me, an oddity in his wheelchair close to the altar and old ladies touch my shoulder, as though I'm holy and can transmit graces though my body.'

Naturally, Margaret wanted him to go to Mass, yet she did not want to force him. It would have been easy to push him to church, but this would have denied him his freedom and self-respect.

So he stopped going to Mass. He was suffering incredible torments, believing his life was useless, without purpose or reason. He had neither peace nor answers within himself.

He was still going to the wheelchair gatherings, arranging transport for the others and getting involved in various ways, but this was just to keep his mind off his inner torment. He would look at his mother in frustration and beg her, 'What am I going to do? What am I going to do? Tell me. You should know.'

But Margaret had no solution, only a quiet desperation gnawing at her heart. It was now a habit for her to turn to Mary, 'You were a Mother too. You suffered through your only Son, so you understand how I don't know what to do to help mine. If he doesn't get straightened out, I know that for the rest of his life, however long it may be, he is going to be like this with a gigantic chip on his shoulder. So please help me. Put words into my mouth. Let me help him to mature properly and not be embittered.'

She knew that, barring a miracle, he could not have much more than a year to live. He was now nineteen. She had come to terms with the fact that he would never walk, never be cured or gain strength. He would just grow weaker and weaker until he died. She could accept all this. What she shrank from was a bitter, frustrated son.

For his part, Eddie had accepted his handicap with all the limitations it imposed on him. He could face up to those but not to a life deprived of peace and stripped of all sense of purpose. He had to receive everything from other people – help, acts of kindness and caring compassion. Was he never to give anything in return? He felt a burden, not only to his family but to the community.

In desperation, he would turn on his radio, only to be plunged further into gloom. It was 1968, the year of violent revolution among the youth in several European cities. Though young Dubliners were not involved, they were affected by youthful hopes being stamped out by elderly European materialism which could brook no demands for renewal or reform. This shattering news simply deepened his crisis with every bulletin, outraging his sense of justice and fair play.

4

Mary's Answer

Two things were clashing, Eddie's deepening despair and
Margaret's undiminished trust in Mary. Eddie was twenty-
one by now and must have felt that his end was near. He
knew he had not been expected to live out his teens. How
then, could he escape the cloud of hopeless frustration that
met him at every turn? Each new attempt to prove himself
and raise his low self-esteem had turned to ashes – study,
music, a job, human love, even his religious faith – all had
turned out to be so many idols with feet of clay. Impossible
to begin to imagine the despair that stares a totally helpless
man in the face. No wonder his mother dreaded more and
more his growing bitterness of soul. How terrible if he were
to die like that without hope even in the future life!

And yet, Margaret was sure that Mary would somehow
find a way and discover a solution to her son's plight. Was
there not that Irish saying, 'If there's a problem, there's a
solution; if there's no solution, there's no problem'?

Mary had found so many solutions in the past fifteen
years, ever since that specialist's cruel prediction, 'You
can't expect him to live out his teens.' Surely, she would
not let her down now.

Faith, hope, trust – call it what you will – has an un-
canny knack of confounding the deadly sceptic. Always,

faith's answer is unexpected. Sometimes, the answer is so surprising and sudden as to astonish even the fervent believer.

So it proved in Eddie's case. Not that there was a sudden miracle. Nor did the answer seem sudden to Eddie. More like dawn creeping over the Alps glimpsed from the air, as the rising sun picks out lakes from mountains, its grey light turning little by little into the radiance of a blood-red disc peeping over the horizon.

The break in the clouds came with a ring on the bell. When Margaret opened the door, she was confronted by a complete stranger, a young man called Tom Sherrard who declared that he had been asked to visit by their mutual friend, Josie Grue in Liverpool. He had come over from London to stay with his mother in Dublin.

Tom and Eddie were soon best friends. Eddie was fascinated by Tom's story which had begun, without his knowledge, some twenty years before. Eddie became more and more intrigued, as he was led in imagination into the air-raid shelters of war-torn Trent in 1943. There, he seemed to be in the company of a twenty-three year old philosophy student, Chiara Lubich, who had taken refuge with her young friends in an unsafe shelter from Allied bombs destroying their homes and their lives. This was Northern Italy's first experience of the destructive power of saturation bombing. Each time the sirens summoned them to the shelter, Chiara armed herself with a copy of the Gospels and a candle. At most she and her friends reckoned they might have a week or two left to live. All their ideals and dreams had collapsed; so they decided to choose God as the only ideal that would survive the bombs. They wanted to put him in the first place in their lives. Not knowing how to do this, they searched the Gospels for an answer.

There they found words that were literally life-giving. The Holy Spirit seemed to be directing them to those words of Jesus that conquer the fear of death to bring new life to birth among his followers. These words seemed to leap from the page.

'Not everyone who says to me, "Lord, Lord", shall enter the kingdom of heaven, but he who does the will of my Father who is in heaven' (Matthew 7:21).

The will of the Father was immediately a ready-made programme for meeting the Lord at death. But what was his will? They found it in Christ's dying command, 'This is my commandment, that you love one another, as I have loved you' (John 15:12).

These girls, who had no time to consult a priest, having to rush to the shelters perhaps eleven times a day, felt that here was the Father's will in a nutshell, containing the summary of all the teaching of Jesus. Here was a practical command to be put into action right away. Jesus had shed every drop of his blood for his followers and here he was ordering them to do the very same. So, in all simplicity, they looked at one another and said, 'I'm ready to die for you, and you, and you,' a real possibility as the bombs rained down.

Eddie was on home ground, as he listened to Tom. He felt he knew quite a bit about death and what it must have been like to face up to it in the shelters. He could easily imagine the girls' surprise at finding themselves still alive, and not only alive, but filled with an incredible joy that took away all fear of the bombs. A surprise that grew as more and more people joined their little group, until their numbers had reached some five hundred in a few months.

Tom had a way of telling their story that made you feel part of it and their surprised joy as they discovered the answers to their bewilderment. Where did this joy come from? And all these people – what drew them? Again they looked in the Gospel and there found the answer they might have guessed all along:

'Where two or three are gathered in my name, there I am in the midst of them' (Matthew 18:20).

Of course! Jesus must be here as he had promised. Was his New Commandment not making them one in his name? He was the one they had chosen, in whose name they begged for mercy whenever they failed to live his words. Not only would he be alive when the bombs stopped destroying their city, but he was strong enough to take away all their fears. Besides, if he was present, brought among them by their mutual love, as they suspected, his very presence would have been strong enough to attract all the other people. Not only was he removing everyone's fear but his New Commandment of Love was inspiring them with unusual generosity, as the rich came to the aid of the poor and the bombed out were welcomed into homes still standing. No wonder Chiara and her friends came to be known as the 'People who spread warmth' or the *Focolarini* (the People of the *Focolare* or Hearth).

What puzzled Eddie was how and when Tom had become caught up in these girls' story. For clearly they were not just people he had heard of, but personal friends with whom he felt a close bond. Tom explained that as the War came to an end, these five hundred men and women, now bound together by strong commitment to Jesus' Words and teaching on community living, had become scattered throughout Italy while remaining true to the life of unity revealed to them in the shelters. Wherever they had gone through the demands of work, fidelity to his Words gave rise to more and more groups living the life discovered first by Chiara and her early companions. After a few years, their Gospel *Ideal of Unity* had leapt over frontiers. By

1960, it had begun to reach England and spread widely throughout the Catholic and Anglican Communions. Tom himself had discovered it through a friend of his who was a monk. It had gradually become clear to him that this was the way God had marked out for him too.

He, in fact, belonged to a group of the Focolare Movement living in London at the centre of what was known as the Zone of Britain and Ireland.

Before he left Dublin, Tom had invited Eddie and Margaret to join a party of English adherents of the Movement, to spend a week together near Rome, learning to live this Gospel way of life. Eddie recalled what happened:

'Tom invited us to take part in an Ecumenical trip they were organising for the following Easter. At the thought of going to Rome, I immediately said yes! My mother agreed too, but with reservations; she wondered how on earth we would surmount all the problems involved in taking me on such a long journey. But Tom kept writing to us from England, explaining how we could arrange it and offering every kind of help – even financial. And in the end we went!'

Months passed quickly and Eddie began to get excited about the trip, not from any religious motivation, but because it was a chance to get away. Margaret thought seriously about the journey, wondering if this could possibly be Mary's answer. It was quite amazing how their difficulties were overcome. The day came, they had the tickets and were ready to go. As they arrived at Dublin Airport, Margaret grew apprehensive. It was almost midnight and they were to fly to Gatwick in England. What would happen if there was no one to meet them? Should they turn back?

Then the forklift was approaching and soon had Eddie high in the air and being wheeled into the plane. The journey had begun! Everything was going well. An ambulance met them at Gatwick to transport them to someone's house. Tea and sandwiches awaited them, and the family had moved a bed downstairs for the night. Not that they slept much. Next morning they were driven to the airport. There was a crowd from all over England, with Josie and her Liverpool friends to greet them. The sight of her was very reassuring.

This time there was no forklift and no one could figure out how to get Eddie on board. The plane could not set off without him and Eddie could not get on. Eventually the two pilots came to his rescue and carried him on. At Rome Airport their new friends had foreseen the difficulty and helped him off. Still Margaret was worried. She knew that two coaches had been laid on to take the English party to their destination, but how was Eddie to get into the coach? This too, had been taken care of. Soon a car was whisking them both to the centre at Rocca di Papa some miles outside Rome in the Alban Hills near the Pope's summer residence at Castelgandolfo. Margaret was delighted. Generally, she had to think of so many things. Now, other people were doing the thinking, and with so much love for them both. Eddie recalled the warmth of their welcome from many young men and women of different nationalities:

'What struck me was the love of everyone there. Nothing was impossible for these friends. A group of boys, trying to live this Christian way of life, looked after me all the time, putting me to bed and getting me up. I remember when I arrived, I noticed that my bed was very soft. I mentioned that I was used to having a board under the mattress. When it was time to go to bed, I found that they had put a door under the mattress. "We took it off a cupboard," they explained. Incidents like this one made a deep impression on me.'

Normally, when Margaret and Eddie went anywhere, they stayed together because he had to be helped at table, since he could not feed himself. But here it was different. He was always with the boys, chatting with them. They pushed him from place to place, helped him in the bathroom and at table. It was all so normal. He felt free instead of being tied to mother's apron strings all the time.

Eddie discovered that he was taking part in an Ecumenical Congress of an unusual kind. Its theme was the discovery of his new friends that 'God is Love', with a concrete love for every human being. This was a fact of life they had only been able to experience when each one of them had decided to make a personal choice of God as Love. This choice led them to put God in the first place in their lives by a united decision to concentrate on his New Commandment, 'Love one another as I have loved you.' This command proved to be the summary of all his teaching. Putting it into practice gradually, they found, meant paying attention to the details of that teaching, such as love of enemies through merciful forgiveness and refusing to judge others. Listening to the many things that were said, Eddie was discovering God in a new way as a loving Father whose very nature is Love. He was becoming a reality, made tangible by the love reaching him through his sons and daughters who made up this community.

Perhaps the high point for Eddie and Margaret was the visit to St. Peter's where the Swiss Guard came to greet them and take them to the high altar to join a small circle of people waiting to meet Pope Paul VI. They were overwhelmed by the splendour of it all in the packed basilica. After the Pope had addressed the assembly, he came to speak with those nearest to him. He came smiling up to Eddie, gave him a rosary and urged him to be patient and keep joy in his heart. He also blessed Margaret and gave her a key-ring bearing the papal arms. The experience left them speechless. They had never dreamt they would be so close to the Pope. Later that day, when Eddie was asked to share his experience in St Peter's, he insisted that the Pope's encouragement to 'Be patient and keep joy in your heart' was for all and not just for him.

The following day they went to the Catacombs. There they had Mass in the church above the underground passages, the very place where the early Christians had gathered for the Eucharist in times of persecution. Eddie had presumed it would be impossible to carry him sixty feet below ground down very steep steps, but his friends said, 'No, Ed! You must see this. There's no problem. We'll get you down.'

Normally he would have been nervous, afraid that the boys would lose their balance or their grip on his chair, but somehow he felt quite safe in their hands. Because of their care for him in the last few days he knew they would not harm him.

They were all astonished that his wheelchair just fitted into the narrow passages with one and a half inches to spare. Eddie laughed and said, 'Look, the first Christians must have known we would come. They built these corridors exactly the same width as the chair.'

An onlooker noticed how he did his best to ease the burden for the others, leaning his head this way and that. He allowed himself to be helped with great humility and love, always making light of the situation without embarrassment to anyone.

Reluctantly, the end of an unforgettable week had to be faced, with the inevitable farewells to new friends. Eddie recalled the effect upon himself:

'Up to this point I had not consciously been living in a very Christian way. Although I was a Catholic, my indifference had even spread to this aspect of my life. I believed in God but I never wanted to go to church. Although I could not, as yet, say what this new way of life was, the whole experience in Rome had been so fantastic, both for my mother and myself, that we wanted to share it with others. I used to say to my mother, "We must do something, we must," and she would reply, "Well, what do you expect me to do? Do you want me to go and stop people in the street?" '

In any case, they had first to submit their Roman experience to John's scrutiny. Margaret recalls that 'he always prided himself as someone who never took anything on face value but always weighed up the pros and cons before he gave an opinion. He used to say he was like the vendor in a bazaar who bit on the coin to establish it was sound before he accepted it. When Ed and I returned from Rome, I suppose you could say we were on a "high" with all we had seen and heard, but John listened and questioned in such a solemn manner.

'As time went on and he met other people involved in the Focolare, he always asked very pertinent questions.'

When Dori, one of Chiara's first companions, came to Ireland, John really grilled her, asking her all sorts of questions about this new way of life – what about the Muslims? What about social justice? Dori was able to share real experiences of reaching out towards other cultures, other Christian denominations and other world religions. The answers he received were very much in line with his own way of thinking. His heart nurtured a deep desire: 'That all may be one.'

Margaret was sure that 'John wouldn't have hesitated to object if he thought that Ed and I were getting involved in a Movement that wasn't sound, but in no way did this ever happen. He recognised that Focolare was "Church" in its widest and deepest sense. With this he was at peace.'

Later that same year, their London friends invited Eddie and his parents to their summer gathering, called a Mariapolis near Manchester. This was a week-long extension of Rome, except that they found the gathering of five hundred people of all backgrounds, ages and races to have a special flavour peculiar to these islands.

The majority had sacrificed their annual holiday to experience what society could become if it was based on sincere living of the Gospel. Each contingent brought its own national flavour as a gift to building up this large community. It was a shock to witness groups from London, Glasgow, Liverpool, Newcastle, Dublin and Belfast mingling and rejoicing in each other's national gifts and actually becoming friends. All ages and backgrounds were learning the art of growing together in unity.

To understand the impact of this English Mariapolis on Eddie and his Mother, we need to take a look at the origins and development of this unique international happening:

It all began in 1949 as the answer to a need within the Focolare Movement. Soon after the war, the Movement began to spread throughout Italy. But then Chiara was advised by her doctor to have a rest. She went with her early companions into the Dolomite mountains surrounding Trent. Their first gatherings were held at a place called Tonadico in the Val di Primiero.

They had a very simple aim – to revive and deepen their commitment to the life of unity which God had revealed to them in the air-raid shelters of Trent. They needed not only to experience again the presence of Jesus in their midst, but to advance with him, allowing him to reveal to them his plans for the future. Not a retreat, then, to a life once known in a happy past, but an advance towards goals as yet hidden from their sight.

These summer gatherings they called the Mariapolis or City of Mary. To their astonishment, each year they found the numbers attending each Mariapolis growing dramatically. So much so that by 1959, 10,000 people came in stages to the single Mariapolis. It became evident that one was not enough. The presence of many non-Italians suggested the need to go beyond Italian frontiers. So the Mariapolis came to be held in many countries, until, in 1986 one hundred Mariapolises were held throughout the world. Today they are held in one hundred and sixty nations. Usually lasting between three days and a week, at some convenient meeting place, each Mariapolis numbers anything from two hundred to two thousand folk.

Eddie and Margaret first met the Mariapolis at Middleton's Hopwood Hall, Manchester, in 1971. Just before they set out for it with the Irish contingent, Eddie opened his heart to Chiara in his first letter to her.

5

City on a Hill

In this letter, Eddie tells Chiara what he owes to her and the Focolare Movement. He describes his first tentative steps at living the lessons of Rome and of his desire for guidance and further training. He thanks her for the news that she is about to send two experienced Focolarine to Dublin and tells of his longing to return to Loppiano which he had visited briefly during his stay in Rome.

Dublin, 19 July, 1971

Dear Chiara,

My name is Edward and I am an Irish Gen.* As I write this letter, everybody who knows about the Movement in Ireland, is pleased to know that two Focolarine are coming to stay in September. At times we have felt cut off and struggled to find unity, but the knowledge of two Focolarine coming to live in Ireland gives us great strength. I know I speak on behalf of everybody when I thank you

---

* Young people who are members of the Focolare Movement, cf. chapter 8.

for giving us such a wonderful gift. We are willing to work hard to live the Ideal of "Jesus in the Midst" but we need plenty of guidance so we can spread our roots deeply.

I would like to tell you my experience of how the Focolare Ideal has helped me. I am twenty-two years of age and I have been confined to a wheelchair for eleven years. Before I had learned about the Ideal, I had accepted my physical disability but rather in a negative way. I accepted it on face value and as the will of God. I accepted it as my fate not to be able to help myself or other people. Now I see things in a different light. I see my disability as a *Gift* from God!

Therefore I now realize my physical limitations and understand my suffering as my strength. That it is all for my sanctification; instead of being a hindrance it is a help! Being physically unable to do things has given me something. I feel I have discovered a new spiritual awakening in myself. Many times I see my friends in need of help and although I cannot help them in a physical way, by loving them and sharing their worries, I can give them spiritual support and share in their joys! And sorrows!

Because of my disability I am unable to visit my friends very often and share in their activities as I would like, but I try to live the Ideal to the best of my ability. I try to see Jesus in whatever I am doing. While behaving in this manner, many times I have had the experience of a friend calling suddenly to my unsuspecting surprise, though I could have despaired at being alone and not being able to visit my friends. But instead I did all that was possible for me to do out of love. Wished my friends well in what they were doing and tried to see Jesus in them. Because of this I was not despairing; I was loving and I was not alone. I was together with a friend.

Thus the Focolare Ideal has helped me tremendously

and provided the bricks to rebuild my life. It has guided me in my search for God's plan for me.

At the moment of writing, I would dearly wish to go to Loppiano to live and train in reciprocal love, though realising this is my will, not necessarily His. So Chiara, I know you can advise me and with your unity help me to find God's plan for me. All I want to do is live the Christian message of love, knowing I have to be like Mary, to become the silence for Christ's words to fall on. But whatever happens, Chiara, I know with your unity I will see God's role for me much more clearly.

All the meetings we have had in Ireland up to now have been held in my house, which has been a great source of joy to my parents and me. On Saturday 24 July, my Mother and I and about fourteen other people from Ireland will be going to the English Mariapolis in Manchester. We are looking forward to it very much and we know that you will be thinking of us and we will be thinking of you.

In Ireland at the moment we are living in exciting times with the growth of the Ideal of Unity and I am pleased to be able to share the joy with you.

Yours in love and unity,

Edward.

That week in Manchester rekindled Eddie's experience of Rome and increased his longing to go to Loppiano, the first of half-a-dozen towns set up as permanent cities of Mary in different continents. These served the dual purpose of training young people of different backgrounds and races to live in harmony, and demonstrate to the thousands of weekend visitors the advantages of Gospel-inspired living. By November, Chiara had replied to Eddie, encouraging him to find a way to reach Loppiano with the help of his London friends, who were able to make his dream come true in 1972. As before, they arranged for him and Margaret to be flown to Italy and be transported by car to Loppiano for a more leisurely stay.

To appreciate the awakening of Margaret and Eddie on arrival in Loppiano, it helps to go back to the early Christian Community in Jerusalem. There, we are told, the disciples brought all their goods and money and laid them at the feet of the Apostles. They held all things in common, no one claiming anything as his own. Yet no one was in need.

That is the conscious aim in Loppiano too. It is a small industrial town raised above Incisa, which lies in the Arno Valley about twelve miles south of Florence on the Autostrada. The land consists of a beautiful undulating table, basking in the Italian sun, within easy reach of Valombrosa which rises majestically to the East, recalling the famous Camaldolese hermit community of St John Gualbert, whose ideal his followers still perpetuate in that place.

The six hundred inhabitants of Loppiano are men and women, mostly young, of all nationalities, drawn from five continents to this haven of peace by all manner of motives and from all walks of life. Each has his own unique adventure to explain his presence there. Some are only passing guests. One of these guests, a huge, jet-black American, had perhaps the strangest story of all. He began life in New York, where his father was murdered. Leaving his mother, the son drifted to Vienna, where he became involved in the underworld. From there he was sent to do a job in Rome where he ran out of money. After an unaccountable two hours on his knees in St Peter's, this unbeliever was hitching his way back to Vienna when he thumbed a lift from a Loppiano car. The boys brought him back with them. After a night's rest, they offered to drive him back to his boss in Vienna. He accepted.

On arrival, he left one of his new friends in a church with the words 'If I'm not back in an hour, don't wait. You'll know you'll never see me again.' Back with his boss, there was hell to pay. His friend prayed. An hour passed, two hours, three hours and still he prayed. After three hours, his American friend tapped him on the shoulder.

'I don't know how I escaped with my life.

'My boss couldn't understand a thing I said, nor why I wanted to change my life. He feared a police trap. In the end he gave in with this warning, "Remember, we've never met." '

Not many Loppiano citizens could match that story perhaps. Besides, our American friend was only a passing guest like Eddie. He stayed several weeks until he had learnt how to live the Christian life of the little town. Other citizens have their own amazing tales. Like the two Irishmen who had set out for Palestine from Dublin in search of God, only to find their search at an end in Loppiano. Or the Buddhist trio, two sisters and a brother, who had been called by God from South Korea. Or, again, Eddie's Chinese friend whose mother and family had escaped with him from Communist China, only to begin his long search for the peace of heart that awaited him in the Focolare house of Hong Kong.

Like all its citizens, Eddie was pleased to find there were no police in Loppiano since the inhabitants were concentrating on the town's single law: 'Love one another as I have loved you'. The only task for the Mayor of Loppiano is to help everyone obey that law.

The most evident work in this town of scattered homes was agriculture, with strong emphasis on the production of an excellent Chianti wine from the extensive vineyards. So it came as a surprise to Margaret and Eddie to find themselves escorted to a variety of modern factories and workshops. Most obvious was the caravan factory which turned out very tasteful homes for the tourist industry. Near that was the large electrical repair shop, reconditioning electric meters for resale.

Most back-breaking of all, perhaps, was the rag shop where thousands of pieces of cloth of all colours and shapes had to be sorted according to kind for recycling.

The men employed in these industries learn after much practice, to labour in a particular way, concentrating with intense application of mind on the work in hand, while their hearts are directed towards the Brother who works among them and alongside them in each neighbour. The fruit of this labour in the spirit of Jesus' New Commandment of love for one another is a rare tranquility charged with the joy of mutual love.

These young men would spend their mornings studying Scripture and the original insights given to all branches of theology by Chiara Lubich's rediscovery of the Gospel message of Unity in Charity. One might call it a new *Summa Theologica*.

So, too, would the young women whose contribution to the economy of Loppiano springs from art work, expressing itself in the mass production of ceramics, painting, sculpture and toys. This work displays the superior originality of ordinary artists working together in unity. This involves each individual's inspiration being pooled until every object is perfected by the united minds and hearts of all, before ever it is created as a separate artifact.

No wonder Eddie and his mother were enthralled by this enchanted place, the first of many such towns that have sprung up in all continents.

Yet Eddie recorded that in the midst of all this joy, he experienced a deep spiritual crisis.

'Loppiano was a wonderful experience and a frightening one. I felt for the first time in my life that I was alone and I had to face up to this. Although Loppiano's life was one of unity and community, it also meant that, alone, you had to make a choice of God and, alone, you had to face him. Nobody else could live your life for you. This frightened me because, although I had tried to face my handicap, I realized now that it was not enough to do this indifferently. It was vitally important for me to face up to it directly and to be happy with my state exactly as I was: To *choose* it.

'Even though in one sense it was frightening, the experience of Loppiano was so wonderful that I would have liked to stay there much longer. When I suggested this to some of the "citizens" of the town, they explained to me that my job was to go back to Ireland and bring this way of life there. A year earlier, I would have been upset by this answer, but now I knew it was right. There in Loppiano everyone had something to offer and I had learnt that I, too, could give something. I had been loved so much that I realized my life was to love. In the past I had not been able to understand why I had to receive all the time and give so little. At Loppiano I had discovered that receiving was giving as well. I had found a job at last and much more. Although I still did not know what it would entail, I had found that my vocation was loving others.'

Like so many hundreds of others who have passed through Loppiano, he emerged with God the victor over his own ego. He chose God as the Ideal of his life, which meant accepting every detail of his will, above all, that of his muscular dystrophy. Perhaps Eddie could never have made that very personal, very private choice anywhere else but Loppiano. Maybe he needed to experience unity with others who had made that same choice, a choice that also caused many of them much anguish before the joy of God's love burst the bubble of their individual selfishness.

Whatever Eddie's case, he experienced a double joy afterwards. One Sunday afternoon, he found Loppiano's natural amphitheatre filling up with some 60,000 young people from all over Europe. They had come to celebrate in mime, song and dance the joy of their united discovery that 'God is Love'. Dressed in the immense variety of their native costumes, they presented their national arts to each other as gifts, each performance a unique contribution to the combined splendour of the feast. Their first experience, perhaps, of the fact that nations and races can be friends as well as individuals, with no need to compete or be enemies.

Perhaps Eddie's mind went back to Eletto whose striking portrait dominated the main building of Loppiano. Pope Paul VI's nephew, Eletto, and his sisters had joined the Focolare Movement in the 1950's. He had inherited Loppiano and made a gift of it, along with his life, to God as a disciple of Chiara. Soon after his donation, he was drowned in a lake in his successful effort to save a young boy adrift in a boat.

This Congress of international song and dance must have seemed to many as the divine response to Eletto's sacrifice.

Whatever the secret of it all, Eddie and Margaret were amazed to find the citizens of Loppiano putting on a farewell concert especially for them on their last night in the town.

Next day they left with full hearts, hoping and praying that Our Lady, whom they were bidden to take with them, would somehow achieve the impossible and use them to make the wonder of Loppiano a reality in Dublin too.

6

A Job at Last

'Ever since I had gone into a wheelchair, in all that time of desperate searching, I had looked to my mother for answers. It was equally difficult for her and all she could do was pray. She continued to do this during the period when I was not praying, when I didn't really believe in God. Now, at Loppiano, we had discovered the solution together. Before we had been one in suffering – now we were one in joy.

'When I arrived back from Loppiano, something happened which I felt was a confirmation of what I had understood there – that my vocation was to love others. At this time I had no job, but I was wondering how I was going to support myself. I had no disability allowance, so my parents were maintaining me. A few months after my return, the law was changed and I became eligible for an allowance. It was a very small amount but for me it was a sign that God *did* want me to have a job – which I was not able to do anyway – and that, therefore, I could concentrate my whole life on this new discovery of love. To prove this, God was even giving me a salary!

'On leaving Loppiano, someone had told me that, just as Mary at the cross had had to leave Jesus to look after John, in the same way I had to leave Loppiano in order to build up in Ireland – amongst those with whom I would come in contact – the life I had discovered in Loppiano!'

Evidently the impact of Chiara Lubich in Rome and of her followers in Loppiano had impressed upon Eddie the great urgency of obeying that parting injunction. But how was it to be done? As Margaret had pointed out, she could hardly go into the street and invite people in. She was not as anxious as Eddie, feeling that if Mary had answered her prayers to find a solution to his deep-seated frustrations, she could hardly refuse his desire to spread her own good news. This was Mary's problem anyway, since her Focolare Movement had long-since claimed the attention of the Vatican which had not hesitated to call it 'The Work of Mary'.

Margaret reminded her son of Chiara's warning not to talk about their discovery back home, since no one would understand who had not shared the same experience. Life before words seemed to be the motto they needed. Chiara had underlined this vital maxim by recounting the story of the young missionary in Pakistan. Having met her in Rome, he could not wait to spread her story everywhere, but fortunately he could not speak the language; so he was forced to care for everyone he met so effectively that at the end of six months his words were accepted with joy.

Another curb to Eddie's impatience was Chiara's own writings, especially her *Meditations* passed on by his London friends. These deep thoughts, the fruit of her experience, not only gave the key to the communal life of places like Loppiano, but revealed the divine strategy behind life's mysterious complexities. Naturally, the whole problem of suffering loomed large on Eddie's horizon. Once he began to accept his own handicap as a gift from God, he became enchanted with Chiara's insight into suffering. All his experience up to this point had led him to look on suffering as a curse. Now he found himself looking upon it, not only as a blessing, but something to be welcomed as a springboard to love or incentive to build the bridge of unity. As Chiara wrote:

We would die if we did not look at you, who transformed, as if by magic, every bitterness into sweetness; at you, crying out on the cross, in the greatest suspense, in total inactivity, in a living death, when, sunk in the cold, you hurled your fire upon the earth, and reduced to infinite stillness, you cast your infinite life to us, who now live it in rapture.

It is enough for us to see that we are like you, at least a little, and unite our suffering to yours and offer it to the Father.
So that we might have Light, you ceased to see.
So that we might have union, you experienced separation from the Father.
So that we might possess wisdom, you made yourself 'ignorance'.
So that we might be clothed with innocence, you made yourself 'sin'.
So that God might be in us, you felt him far from you.

Cf. *Meditations*, New City, London, 1989, p.30

Since Chiara's whole experience of the building of unity sprang from the bitter suffering of war, her followers had repeatedly witnessed the power of love, not only to transform suffering but to allow God to turn hostile environments into havens of peace. Could he not also use Eddie's handicap for his own purposes? Eddie felt that this could indeed happen, since Chiara was also revealing to him that every suffering is accompanied by the mysterious presence of Jesus Forsaken on the Cross. In every pain, desolation, despair and sin we encounter him who cried out to his Father, 'My God, My God, why have you forsaken me?', the cry of everyone who asks the question, 'Why should this happen to me?' Had he not been asking 'Why?' all through these long years of frustration? Dare not he, too, like Chiara and her friends, give a name to each day's quota of suffering?

Jesus himself, seemed to be inviting him to share his cross of handicap with him, since he had already paid for every painful moment of it, even to feeling in his own heart Eddie's bewildering frustration. Could he do other than embrace this incredible friend, this Jesus Forsaken as the very spouse of his soul?

As he learnt to greet every pain, every setback as the shadow of the cross, he was learning to welcome his friend who hung upon it.

Jesus had promised that he would reveal himself to the person who loved him (John 14:21). Eddie and Margaret needed time to absorb all he was revealing to them. There simply had to be this gap before the start of the Gospel revolution in Dublin. If it was to happen at all, it had to begin with them. The new Gospel tree that was about to be born, had to put down strong roots. Not that they had long to wait for God to act, once he was sure of those roots. Made present by their mutual love, he began to use his age-old implement, the cross.

Let Eddie recall. 'A few months after my return to Ireland, I met another boy who had come across this same way of life. We kept in touch in every possible way, phoning each other and meeting as often as we could. We did not know what was going to happen – all we knew was that we had discovered something important to us. Jesus says that where two or three are gathered in his name, he will be there among them, and although we knew very little about this way of life, we experienced something of these words because we came to know and understand each other completely, which humanly is not possible.

'Some friends of mine knew of a girl who had the same handicap as myself and who was very depressed. They thought that I might be able to help her, and so they introduced us. Her name was Marian. I found that she was going through the same stage that I had gone through at the age of about eight or nine, although for her it was probably worse as she was older and less able to cope with it than I had been. She was very closed in and unable to talk about her disability. I was helpless, not knowing what to do, and yet, regularly once a week or once a fortnight, she would come to see me. There was nothing I could do, I could just love, just be there. Gradually, she became more open and came with me to some meetings where she discovered the new way of life that I had discovered. Afterwards, however, she seemed to show little interest. Nevertheless, although she was still frightened to talk about her disability, she kept on coming to see me. I felt that something must be affecting her, although I could see no evidence of it, and that I had to go on loving without expecting that anything would come of it.

'In the end, she realized that the Christian way of life I had discovered was everything for her too. After attending an international congress for young people, she said she had found a new life. Since she could play the guitar, together we wrote some songs. I would write a few words based on an experience of mine and show them to her. A few days later she would experience something similar and complete the song. These were not just songs but something of our lives. They were all about suffering and yet they were really happy. God had brought something beautiful out of our suffering and we could show this in beautiful terms. We realized that suffering does not end in itself; you have to get over it and embrace it and then you discover a joy beyond, which is the only thing that lasts.'

Marian has kept a precious birthday card from Eddie expressing this joy. Written in 1977 or 78, it shows how deep their unity was growing right up to his death; it reads:

'I could not forget you on your birthday, so to prove this, here is my card. It's a very special feast that remembers another expression of His love (You!). Thank you for remaining in this Love!

All my love, *Eddie (Radix)*.'

Eddie also recalled how this unity began to produce fruits: 'This girl's younger brother, Pádraic, was impressed and attracted by the change in her, so he began to come and see me, to find out more for himself. I was able to share everything I had learned with him. He was only fourteen and I was twenty-six. Humanly speaking we had nothing in common, and yet, by living this life of mutual love, a wonderful relationship was built up between us, and he joined the group of boys that had begun with just two of us'. Pádraic was also learning the guitar from his sister and with time all three joined in composing songs which have stood the test of time.

Pádraic Gilligan's friendship with Eddie was special. It began when he was fourteen in his second year at high school, lasted for five years and went through deepening stages. Pádraic would visit Eddie every Saturday for a couple of hours which he combined with a part-time job in an off-licence. At first, they would talk about sport, school and this job, Eddie taking special care to read up the sports news to share with his young friend. 'From the very start, there was a very good relationship between us. Eddie looked a bit older than his twenty-six years because of his beard and handicap.

'When I came to know the Focolare through my sister, Marian, our relationship changed gear in a way. Eddie responded to this new thing in my life and he began to take me on a journey through his life before and after he met the Movement – his frustrations before and his discoveries in Rome and Loppiano. When he realized I was trying to live the Gospel, he began to prepare talks on specific topics to share with me, taking me through all the facets of the Gospel Ideal of unity, week by week. Insensibly we moved on to telling each other our experiences during the previous week, he with Margaret and John and the members of the group of young people living the Ideal, his Gen Unit, that met in his house – and I mine with Marian and my parents, at school and in my little job. The deeper our relationship grew, the more our experiences focused on living the Word of Life* and generating the presence of Jesus between us.

'As I grew older, I would drop in on Eddie more frequently (after school) during the week. I felt very much part of the family. Margaret and John were tremendously hospitable. I loved her currant-buns and queen-cakes which often went into my pocket when her back was turned. I was fascinated by John and we had deep discussions on current affairs and all sorts of topics. So I was very much part of the family but Eddie was the main reason for my visits to be inspired by all he had to share of the Ideal.

---

* It is a practice of the Focolare Movement worldwide to take one verse from Scripture a month and put it into practice, as a way of evangelizing the whole of life.

'The relationship I had with Eddie essentially was real. Eddie was my best friend. I shared everything with him. When I was in school I would think frequently of him. I would count on his unity, I knew where he was, I knew he was always there and if things were difficult in school or if I was finding myself being drawn into situations which were contrary, let's say, to what living the Ideal would require, I'd think of Eddie, I'd think of him specifically in his room at home where I knew he would most likely be and I would be able to draw strength from the knowledge that we had Jesus in the midst at a distance. That was a phenomenal experience to have as a teenager, to come in contact with a person who became a true friend and who was able to show me the dimensions of true friendship.

'When I think back, as a thirty year old now, who teaches religion to sixteen year olds, I can see clearly what I was like at sixteen. I was looking for friendship in the same way as the sixteen year olds I now teach; they are looking for a deeper friendship than the slap in the back camaraderie that exists between sixteen year old boys. They are deeply searching for meaning, for something that will last and I just feel very privileged to have found that in my relationship with Eddie. My relationship with Eddie was not just two people who liked each other coming together, it was two people who were trying to love each other as brothers in Christ.'

7

As I Have Loved You

Mother and son had been fired with a strong desire to spread Chiara's family throughout Ireland. They felt that her Ideal of unity according to the teaching of Jesus would help solve many problems, and bring a new source of hope to the troubled North.

As we have seen, they had no idea how to begin or what to do. Eddie was perhaps more anxious than his mother to get started. After all, he had been commissioned to spread Chiara's message in his own home city of Dublin. The life of Loppiano simply must be given a chance.

Fortunately, Margaret and Eddie had not been dazzled by the amazing fruits of the life of unity – international co-operation on a vast scale, new solutions to ancient social and racial problems, the world of politics, medicine, teaching and industry penetrated at last by Gospel values – all this and more demonstrated in the astonishing harmony of Loppiano where Eddie now longed to become a permanent citizen.

They were particularly impressed by a moment of decision in the lives of Chiara and her first companions. Struck by the prayer of Jesus 'That they may all be one; even as you, Father, are in me and I in you, that they also may be in us, so that the world may believe that you have sent me' (John 17:21), they had offered themselves as the fulfilment of that prayer. They wanted to be the living embodiment of his desire that 'All may be one'.

This insertion of their lives into the very life of the Holy Trinity seemed to be the heart of the matter. As in the early days in Trent, Margaret and Eddy must become in Dublin the visible sign of the unity of the Three in One.

But how are Jesus and his Father one? In love. In the Holy Spirit, who is their mutual Love. No wonder Jesus had given his disciples this unique badge of discipleship. He who is Love will return on earth among his disciples if they have love one for another.

Christians down the ages had always paid lip-service to this commandment, but they had observed it mostly in the breach. What had been the outcome? Had not Gandhi turned away in sadness, saying, 'Why should I become Christian? Christians are always fighting.' How ironic that this great apostle of peace who used to speak to his millions of followers in the words of Jesus himself, was blinded to the truth of Christianity by the warring followers of Jesus! No wonder Christian warriors had driven the world of the twentieth century further and further towards atheism until it tottered for decades on the brink of self-destruction. How true Chiara's wry comment, 'our world is geared to war, programmed for war!'

So it was borne in on Margaret and Eddie that their love for each other had to change gear. *They* could not spread the Gospel Ideal of unity. Only *Jesus* could do that, but he needed them for Dublin and Ireland. Ever since their first visit to Rome they had longed to share their treasure, their pearl of great price, with their friends and neighbours, but nothing had happened. Now, after Loppiano where they had offered their lives to Jesus for Ireland, their love underwent a subtle change.

60

They noticed that the command of Jesus had a particular, supernatural nuance they had missed before. They had overlooked the very nature of the love he demanded from his disciples. 'By *this* shall everyone know that you are my disciples . . ., if you have love for one another' (John 13:35). He had commanded them to love '*as I have loved you*'. How had Jesus loved them? By shedding every drop of his blood for them.

Looking at one another, mother and son realized that their love had not yet risen to his level, that ultimate expression of love. 'Greater love has no one than this that he lay down his life for his friends' (John 15:14).

Now, mutual love was the very stuff of their life together, from the moment Margaret woke him in the morning till she bade him 'goodnight'. Her whole life was one of service to Eddie; his life one of acceptance of her minute attention to his constant needs, sacrifice given and sacrifice received.

How could they increase the intensity of their love? Quite simply by changing its object. Had not Jesus said that anything we do to the least of his brothers, we do to him (Matthew 25:40)? Supposing Margaret were to offer all her service to the person of Jesus living in Eddie instead of stopping short at Eddie himself? Supposing Eddie were to receive all her service from Jesus living in Margaret instead of just from Margaret herself?

If that subtle, unseen change were allowed to enter their mutual love, would that not be a gigantic leap forward in their lives? Jesus had said, 'Where two or three are gathered in my name, there am I in the midst of them' (Matthew 18:20).

Had he been waiting all this time to be released, to be allowed to live in 40 Lower Dodder Road, no longer as a prisoner in its three inhabitants, but as a fourth person, alive and active in their local community? True, it was taking John Neylon longer to see the point, but that did not matter. Margaret and Eddie could love Jesus in John too, content to let Jesus work at the best speed for John. All Jesus needed was two people. He was happy to wait for three or more.

But Margaret and Eddie could get started right away. It is difficult to reconstruct what actually happened, but Eddie has left us an account of the moments in those first months after Loppiano that stood out in his memory. A sure sign that their long-awaited guest had taken up residence in their home, is that those moments concerned the first three people Jesus added to their number. Following Eddie's story is like a repetition in miniature of the early days in Jerusalem after the first Pentecost – 'And the Lord added to their number, day by day those who were being saved' (Acts 2:47).

Eddie has already told us about those first three, but they were not alone. Others were joining fairly rapidly. As they were learning from him how to live in unity, he was learning some sharp lessons from Our Lord who was gradually showing him his definite role in the community, as he now tells us:

'Some members of our group were invited to go and represent us at an international congress. When we heard about this a few weeks in advance, I set my heart on going – I felt that it was important that I should be there at all costs, even though at the back of my mind I thought that maybe I was not meant to go. As the time grew close, nobody said "No" – I had to make up my own mind. A few days before we were due to leave, the final decision had to be taken and, as I spoke to a friend who was helping to organize the journey, although he did not say I could not go, I could tell from what he said that it was not the right thing. For a few minutes this was very painful. Suffering had been building up inside me because, deep down, I had known all the time that I would not be able to go, but I had still not faced up to it.

'I felt terribly upset. It was not fair. Too much was being asked of me. But I had learned that we do not need to be told what the will of God is for us – each of us knows it in our own hearts. In that moment I read something from the Gospel and this calmed me. I suddenly felt a great joy, because I realized that if I had gone, it would all have been ruined because I would have gone for the wrong reasons, and I would not have loved at all. In this realization I rediscovered God.

'It is possible for me to take part in many things because people will always help me, but it is not essential. My role is not something physical, as physically I can do very little. I just have to love and be there for everyone else – without travelling all over the place.

'My life today is a new discovery all the time. Every day somebody is going here or there and I would like to go with them. I feel this and they feel it too. It is good if I can go, but it is something extra – it is not the essential thing. I have discovered that, if I was not in a wheelchair, my life would be very difficult. Maybe I would not even know God, because I would not want to know him. I know that this is the will of God for me, and because of this I can do so many things and reach the deepest level in everything. Only by accepting the will of God and going along that path can I really live a full life, and my life is full.

'I have realized that my task is to be the root of a tree – giving the tree support. This is God's role for me. In our group we are all moving towards God as individuals, but also together. Each of us has a different place – some are at college, some work. My place is always to be here for them. Some of us have to be roots, and some of us have to be branches with a visible and active part. I have to be more "underground". This is hard, but perhaps the branches feel the same. Every part is equal, because each performs a task.

' "God has chosen what is foolish in the world to shame the wise, and has chosen what is weak in the world to shame the strong." Perhaps my life seems foolish to the world. People ask me, "What do you do all day?" "You must be lonely," they say. I cannot explain to them that here at home I do so many things. There are people calling all the time – boys in the group – others who know something or very little of our way of life, or who need help or friendship. I phone; I write letters; my whole life is loving. People say, "Isn't it terrible what life has done to you? How can you be so happy?" All I can do is smile, because I cannot explain, and perhaps it is not important to explain. Maybe it is important to look foolish so as to shame the wise.'

8

New Generation

By 1966 a new generation of the Focolare Movement had come to maturity with a strong desire to unite the young people of the world. Quite naturally, Eddie's growing group joined this army of small units scattered throughout the world whose motto is 'Youth for a united world'.

This youngest branch of the Focolare Movement is known as the Gen Movement, Gen standing for New Generation. It is significant that this branch came into being just before 1968, the year of youthful revolt against the injustice and complacency of older generations whose lives had been dominated by conflict.

Unfortunately, the young revolutionaries in Paris, Berlin, London, Milan and Tokyo tended to spread the areas of conflict by turning the generations against each other. In the midst of all the confusion, the Gen were working quietly for the cause of unity. It was from them that Eddie and his friends learnt the secret of a different revolution.

On fire with his desire to make Loppiano a reality in Dublin, Eddie came to realize that the Gen revolution also involved violence, but violence against his own selfishness rather than against society. This anti-self violence demands a willingness to learn to think and feel with new minds and hearts transformed by the mind and heart of Christ himself. Coming from a world of Love to a world deformed by hate, he, the very Word of God, came to bring new divine words that would refashion the human minds and hearts of those willing to accept them.

Eddie learnt that the words of Jesus are truly *Words of Life* which not only give men and women his way of thinking and feeling but actually give new impetus to every facet of life. They do this not just because they are *his* words but because, in a mysterious way, they actually make him present when put into practice in the detailed circumstances of daily living.

So Eddie came to love the different Words of Life sent to him each month from London. Every month Chiara would choose a new word from the Gospel and put it into practice with her companions well in advance of the Movement. Their experiences of living the Word together enabled her to write a commentary on the monthly Word with suggestions as to how to put it into practice. This was sent out in twelve languages all over the world. This commentary was the fruit of life lived in Our Lord's presence rather than of study. He, made present by their mutual love, became their Master and Teacher.

As Eddie learnt to live the Word in this way, he recalled his experience in Rome and Loppiano of the power of the Word to change his inner life from one of torment over his handicap into one of joyful acceptance of this very special and personal gift from God. Only now, this change was bringing a deeper and more powerful relationship with his parents, something that was not only growing stronger but was, surprisingly, attracting more and more young people to his home. At last, his great desire to spread the flame of 'A United World' was being fulfilled. To learn what actually happened, it is best to ask those members of what became known as Eddie's 'Gen unit' who are still with us.

To read their different stories is like being introduced to the spokes of a wheel. Each member of his unit had an equally close bond with Eddie, the hub, who took the strain of each one's burden and felt it as his own. As a wheel turns, each spoke takes the weight of the whole for that fraction of the turn to which its section of the circumference is subjected. To appreciate something of the ceaseless burden upon the hub, one has to picture the thrust from each spoke reaching the hub as a continual load.

Once Eddie had fully understood his task in the Dublin community, he opened up his mind and heart with tireless generosity to share each person's private worry or individual agony. In fact, we find his friends revealing him as a remarkable counsellor, despite his total lack of training. Intuitively, he had grasped that the essence of counselling is to listen with love. It was his loving silence that somehow opened hearts, relieved tensions and allowed people to find solutions to their own problems.

Alan McGuckian, one of his closest friends, recalls:

'I had the privilege of being very closely involved with him on a number of occasions and so had an extra appreciation of his handicap. I had the task of staying with him throughout the day and also sometimes at night. He had hardly any power in his hands or arms and could only move his head a few inches from side to side. Otherwise he was totally helpless and needed to have everything done for him. Even at night, if his position in bed caused him discomfort, as the same position held for many hours naturally would, he was unable to move even his arm, without help from someone. It is almost impossible for an able-bodied person to appreciate the extent of the helplessness of someone in Eddie's position.

'He had no privacy. For me to witness his humility, patience and simplicity of heart as he had to be helped in everything, even in the most personal ways, was the most powerful experience of my life. The miracle of Eddie's life was that this man who was physically totally helpless, was a *rock* of love, kindness and support to all who knew him. Having lost, as one might think, everything, he was always ready to lose more. As he was confined to his home each day, he used to love the opportunity to go out to the meetings we held in the University at lunch time. As long as there was a car available and a few strong men to lift him in and out, Eddie could come.

'I remember one period when none of us could get a loan of a car for a few weeks and so Eddie had to be left at home. Very often people who can bear great sufferings, lose their patience with relatively minor irritations. Eddie cheerfully saw God's will in this further deprivation. If and when he felt depressed by it all, he never imposed it on the rest of us but went on smiling and encouraging.

'At the Mariapolis, Eddie showed me how he understood that helping him could be a real act of love. He was happy to let others help him and a few times he suggested that I let some other person take over pushing the wheelchair or staying with him, because he felt that to give them this opportunity to love was a gift. He was a genius in the art of loving, even knowing how to turn receiving into giving.

'He tried to love in every situation, in whatever way was called for. He didn't even shirk pointing out when something was amiss. I can sometimes be very careless of my dress and appearance and Eddie a few times pointed out my defect in this regard, but he did it with a frankness and a concern that so obviously came from love that no offence could be taken and improvement always resulted.'

Somehow Pat Delaney came across the Movement and got to know Eddie very well, eventually joining his unit. He recalled how he overturned his whole idea of friendship:

'As most of my spare time was spent in the pub, getting drunk or playing football at the weekends, I found it strange, even embarrassing, listening to people talking about love. I could never understand why fellows I was friendly with in the pub the night before, never seemed to want to continue the friendship. At the Mariapolis I found something new: people with whom I had an instant and very deep relationship. Afterwards I kept in touch with Eddie . . . You couldn't but be impressed by Eddie, he was so simple. I suppose you could say there was the presence of Jesus in his bungalow, a unique relationship between Margaret and Eddie. You know he was always up, or let's put it like this – he was never down.'

Pat seems to have been the first member of Eddie's unit, the person with whom he had a closer bond than with anyone else, the one he described for us on his return from Loppiano. By December, 1973, Pat had made another friend who had job difficulties of the opposite kind to his own. He had to attend many social functions which were little more than heavy drinking sessions. The atmosphere at work became more and more strained, increasing the nervous tension of Gerard's introverted nature. That Christmas his sufferings were greatly increased by the death of an aunt to whom he was very attached. It was shortly after her death that he made friends with Pat. It was a case of the attraction of opposites. Gerard recorded:

'It was great with Pat. He seemed to care in a special way. I just couldn't believe that anyone would want to take an interest in me. He was involved with meals-on-wheels at College and invited me to go around there to help out on Saturdays. One Saturday, in particular, he asked me to meet some friends of his after meals-on-wheels.

'These turned out to be Eddie, Margaret and John. You just had to be impressed by them. I knew a lot of good people, but this was different. It was always special. Margaret always baked a lot and we sat about chatting and getting to know one another. It was very exciting for me. I couldn't believe that people were taking an interest in me.'

Gradually Gerard's painful introspection gave way to positive caring for others – a good example of the truth that 'perfect love casts out fear'. That summer, it became a habit for him to visit Eddie, so that he did not take too much persuasion to take part in a Gen Congress in Rome where his commitment was strengthened:

'I was really converted there. Summer 1974 was really brilliant with Ed. Many Gen from abroad came to stay with him all summer. There was nothing embarrassing about being with Ed and there could have been. He was so alive. I could not think of him as someone handicapped.'

Meanwhile, Pat Delaney, on vacation from College, took two other friends, Brendan Gallagher and Pádraic Smyth, to Canada to earn money. He first talked this move over with Eddie who advised:

'Well, don't talk about our way of life when you're away. Just live it, and later you can tell them about it. Don't say anything; first of all you must live it.'

During their three months in Canada, Eddie kept in close touch, supplying Pat with the monthly Word of Life and *New City*, the Focolare magazine.

Pat reported that his two friends were anxious to know about this Eddie who was always writing to him and where the magazine came from. They had noticed a change in Pat and the new way he had of looking at life. To satisfy their curiosity, he told them a little about the Focolare and promised to take them to meet Eddie back in Dublin. Brendan could hardly wait to meet him.

As Eddie's circle of friends grew, visiting his home in a continuous stream, John's cup was full to overflowing. Margaret pictures him in those days. He was the soul of hospitality.

'The very many Gen boys from Dublin and Belfast always remember the love and openness with which John met them, encouraged them and helped them in whatever way he could.'

Though he was one hundred per cent in tune with Margaret and Eddie, he never felt the need to join any particular branch of the Focolare Movement. He looked upon himself as a 'world man' and applauded its world dimension.

At his funeral in December 1990, Father Brendan Purcell told his countless friends, 'In John's home, many of us here today, who were formerly unaware of each other, indifferent to each other, began to learn how to be a family. John always wanted his house to be open to everyone and, like a welcoming Clare farmhouse, it became a hearth for hundreds of neighbours who felt they belonged there and often dropped in. What happened was more than just the growth of a human family, something even deeper and more lasting. It was the beginning of a big family united in God's love. Without John, we would never have known what a real Christian family community was.'

Eddie could not believe what was happening. Quite suddenly his prayer to be used to spread the 'Good News' of unity in Ireland was being answered and at some speed. Scarcely were Pat and Brendan Gallagher joining their weekly meetings than three lads from Belfast needed lodgings to be with them at least once a month. Once again,

Eddie's home was the only possibility. It was imperative that he welcome them, since they were alone in the North where they had met the Movement through Sister Anna, an Anglican nun loved by all shades of opinion and loyalty. Their only hope of growing in the life of unity was to come South to Dublin and meet with Eddie and his friends on the other side of the border.

So, out of the blue, his unit was born, eight or nine strong almost from birth. Already it had built a double stranded bridge over the two great divides – South and North, and Protestant and Catholic within the North itself. As Eddie must have thought with greater conviction than ever, 'All this was humanly impossible'. If it took God to bring about his friendship with Pat Delaney and Pádraic, Marian's brother, how much more this whole group whose members were unknown to each other so short a time before!

9

The Vanishing Root

Ever since his return from Loppiano, Eddie had felt his bond with Chiara growing stronger each year, until in May '74 he took a decisive step. Like countless others whose fidelity to the life of the Gospel had deepened their unity with her, he wrote to her as his spiritual mother requesting a special gift that would boost his determination to grow in the Christian life.

Dublin, 27 May, '74.

Dear Chiara,
   ... Now, I would like to tell you something which I have felt for quite a while. About two years ago I was in Loppiano. I stayed there for two weeks. Though only there for such a short time, I became part of that City of Mary. Though I could not work, being physically disabled, I played my small part in the Work of Mary. I became part of Loppiano and Loppiano became part of me. While there, I also saw some of your tapes on Jesus Forsaken which were very beautiful. During my stay, the thing that really entered my heart – quite strongly it struck me – was that you were my Spiritual Mother because you

had given your life for God and he gave you the Ideal of unity to share with us and like a true Mother you gave us your everything, your all.

So, like a true son, maybe you could give me a new name or a Word of Life, since I have been born again into a new life of love with you, the first Focolarini, the Gen and everyone who lives that Ideal.

I am in a wheelchair and not strong physically, so I spend a lot of time at home with my Mother. We have a very strong unity together. My role is not in action but in always being here, trying to love and do His will. As Dori once told me, I am the root that stays in the ground. Sometimes it is very *hard* being the root. I want to play the active role – having the enthusiasm of any young person of twenty-five. Yet, I am happy knowing that the Father has a special love for me (as for all of us) and so a special work to do for him; and though sometimes it is full of sorrow, I can always be close to him and the Trinity, which is really all joy.

At the moment, four of us Gen boys are slowly building up Jesus in the midst. The joining of three other boys with me and our mutual desire to have Jesus among us, are, I feel, the fruit of trying to be the root and confirm the will of God for me.

Dear Chiara, I hope I have not tired you too much with my long letter – so I will close now. If you think it is right, I would be very happy with a new name or a Word of Life from you.

From your son in Jesus. One in Mary. *Eddie (McCaffrey)*.
P.S. Greetings also from the other Irish Gen. Pat, Pádraic and Gerard.

By October, Chiara had confirmed Dori's intuition about Eddie's role.

'Dear Eddie,

Please forgive me for not answering sooner to tell you how happy I was to receive your letter.

'Yes, Eddie, God has a very special love for you and Mary has chosen you as one of her privileged children. This is the true wisdom of the cross that the world cannot understand.

'To help you to remain faithful to this special calling, I have chosen for you the Word of Life: "But God chose what is foolish in the world to shame the wise" (1 Cor. 1:27), and the new name: "RADIX", which means "Root".

'I am with you, Radix. My warmest greetings to you and to the other Irish Gen.

In God who is Love. *Chiara*.'

A year later, Eddie thanked Chiara for her presence at all the meetings his Irish friends had attended in Rome, adding:

'I thank you also for the Word of Life and new name you gave me. They became so much part of me, as if I had always had them, that I forgot to thank you for them. Now I feel the revolution of Love inside me, I can really begin and become the 'root', not only for Ireland but for the whole Work of Mary.

Ciao, Chiara. One in Jesus Forsaken, *Radix*.'

The importance of Eddie's new name made his friends think more deeply about his role in the community. One of these, Christopher Connor, had always thought of him as the source of new life springing up in Dublin, striking deeper roots year by year. He first became aware of his growth when he took his down-and-out friend, Jim, to visit him.

'Jim was engrossed in his own problems, seeing no way out. I took him along for perhaps an hour. Eddie said very little but just let him know that he was loved. Coming away, Jim was silent for a while. Then, looking up, he said, "Well things aren't too bad are they?" I had noticed for the first time Eddie's power in weakness and the truth of St. Paul's words, "God has chosen what is weak in the world to shame the strong." '

Chris had also noticed Eddie's need to grow spiritually within himself at the time he received his new name. He was pleased to note the special boost he received that same year:

'I stayed in Dublin until September, 1974. Eddie's progress continued impressively. Probably the biggest single influence in that progress occurred when he began to receive Holy Communion every day. Until then, in my opinion, he lacked a deep, interior life. He understood, of course, the Focolare Ideal of unity through mutual love and lived it in an impressive way. But there was a need for a deeper personal union with God in prayer. That began to change when, in the summer of 1974, two young men from Loppiano talked with Eddie about the need for a deeper unity with each other through the Eucharist. If he were to receive Communion every day, not only would they have a stronger bond with each other but above all he would be deepening his unity with God.'

This looked like a pipe-dream. As things stood, many years before the introduction of lay Eucharistic ministers, he was fortunate to receive Holy Communion once a month from the busy parish clergy. But with God all things are possible to united prayer. And so it proved when his mother asked the local priest to bring him the Sacrament once a week. Three others were delighted to join the team to take care of the remaining six days. One of these priests, Father Anthony McHugh, a much loved Redemptorist, specialized in helping religious with psychological problems. On his weekly visit, he would sometimes be accompanied by a few of his clients. Filing silently into his bedroom, they would bow to Eddie and gather kneeling round his bed. Father McHugh insisted that meeting Eddie helped them to see their problems in perspective. 'He makes me feel like a bloomin' shrine', quipped Eddie.

Another of these priests, Brendan Purcell, had first come across the Movement in Czechoslovakia during the height of the persecution of the Churches there. He was delighted to discover it had taken root in Dublin too. Chiara had, in fact, sent Aurea and Mary to live in Eddie's home in 1972, while they looked for a flat of their own.

Brendan first met them and Eddie in 1973. He recalls, 'I remember the shock the first time I went to shake hands with him to find I had to do all the shaking! I was struck by the extraordinary welcome he gave me. He made me feel glad I had come and immediately wanted to know how things were with me. This characteristic greeting of everyone quickly dispelled any prejudice I might have had about his handicap. He showed me how to see the person, not the handicap. It was just irrelevant. He was so completely lacking in self-consciousness that he appeared not to notice it himself. Looking back, I believe that of all the people I have known personally, Eddie was perhaps the most whole, the most fulfilled and happy.'

Brendan had begun teaching philosophy in University College Dublin in 1972. During his second year, he was asked to help a group of young people involved with the Student Christian Movement. At the weekly meetings, he would share Gospel experiences from *New City* magazine as a way of introducing the monthly Word of Life. Before these meetings he would ring up Eddie to ensure his unity about the programme. They both had in mind Our Lord's promise, 'If two of you agree on earth about anything they ask, it will be done for them by my Father in heaven. For where two or three are gathered in my name, there am I in the midst of them' (Matthew 18:19-20).

Once he was certain of Eddie's unity, even at a distance, Brendan knew that Jesus would be in the midst of the students, giving his light to the receptive crowd who gathered each week. This light was so strong that the thirteen who committed their lives to the Ideal of unity, are still spreading it in various parts of the world.*

Whenever a car could be found, Eddie would join in these meetings but more especially when one of the chaplains at U.C.D. asked Brendan and his friends to sing at student Masses from time to time. He recalls that ill-health once kept Marian away for a week. This was the opportunity to compose a song with Eddie to share with the students on her return. Called 'Always One', it was inspired by Marion and Eddie's experience that they existed for one purpose only, namely to love.

Always One

I want to do so many things,
I want to give my best to You,

---

* Those who found their vocations within the Focolare Movement were: Pat Delaney, David Hickey, Pádraig Gilligan, Paul O'Hara, Robbie Young, Pádraig Smyth, Ita Lyng who entered Focolare; Gerard Mulligan, Marian Gilligan, Rachel Long, Angela Manning who joined the branch of the Volunteers; Alan McGuckian and Tony Bisset who became religious. There were many others who remained as adherents or sympathizers of the Movement. Ita gave her life for Africa. She died, in 1989, among the Bangwa tribe in Cameroon.

But the only thing You ask for
Is my love.

You brighten up my darkest moments
With a love so true,
You make me want to love You only
All day through.

And even though I've really nothing,
I give it all to You,
'Cause I exist
only to love You.

And as I look around I see
Your image in the smiling faces
Of the people who are gathered
in Your name.

I know You are with me always
And my love for You
Is growing stronger with each dawning
When I remain in You.

And only when I become nothing
Am I all in You
'Cause I exist,
only to love You.

Soon after Aurea and Mary left Eddie's home, they were joined by Pina, an Italian Focolarina of long experience. She soon found work in the University as secretary to the Italian Department. Her presence greatly strengthened the unity among the students at the meetings, since she helped to plan them beforehand with the small core-group, although she did not attend the meetings herself. It also meant that the centre of the Movement shifted from Eddie's home to the girls' Focolare, which became the source of life for the rapidly expanding community. This entailed further sacrifice on Eddie's part, a sacrifice mingled with his joy at the expansion of the Movement throughout Ireland.

Throughout this period, and during the rest of the time he knew him, Brendan learnt so many things from Eddie that it is difficult to record them all. Perhaps the most outstanding was his realistic love of Jesus Forsaken whom he epitomized in his own person. He expressed him in his very being, in the uniqueness of his unrepeatable character. He thought of Jesus on the cross as the key, the key to all life's problems, the key to mankind's agonized questioning, in his terrible cry from the cross, 'Why have you forsaken me?' embracing the 'Why?' of every human being and giving it meaning. Eddie's infectious joy and his notorious sense of humour proclaimed that Jesus Forsaken had become the spouse of his soul, since the Father's answer to the anguished question of his Son was the enormous joy of his rising from the dead. Eddie had learnt that Jesus Forsaken, embraced with love in his own person, transformed every sorrow into joy.

All this was borne in on Brendan whenever he mislaid the key of his Honda 50, a not infrequent occurrence. As he trudged the miles back to where he kept his spare, he would recall Eddie's song, 'The Key', and be filled with joy. For, though he had lost his material key, he had found life's Key just like Eddie.

The Key

Every door has closed on me
Except the door to You.
Father, You have shut off everything.
Many dreams, plans and schemes
I've had to lose
So You could be the only one
For me.

You open wide Your arms to me
Offering love consistently
Now I hold the key to You.
It's been so hard to find,
Couldn't see I had it
All the time.

Now I see Your love for me
As something always new.
I turn my key and find
You're always there.
Every day in every way
I have to smile
Realizing You are in each guise.

I open wide my arms to You
And You fill all my emptiness
From your wounds.
It's now no longer I who live
But You who live in me,
Born again for each of us
Through love.

Brendan believes Eddie gave him a special understanding of the place of the sacraments in life. Every Sunday he would offer Mass in his home, bringing him Communion on Mondays and the Sacrament of Reconciliation once a month. 'I think I learnt the real meaning of the Mass from Edward and the crowd of Gen who joined in on Sundays. He prepared and received the Eucharist with such care and above all love, that he was already building the little church, the little Jesus in the midst within which the sacraments were being administered. They were the fruit and crown of the life he was living. At these Masses, we'd always sing the most popular Focolare songs of the time, along with whatever new song had been written by Marian, Eddie and Pádraic. Looking back now, I realize that what was going on was a re-enactment of the New Testament times of the Church. People living the Word and proclaiming the new life it provoked in songs and hymns. These then became the patrimony of the Church, incorporated into the Liturgy and permanent texture of her life.'

Like many others, Brendan brought people he thought Eddie could help to Dodder Road. One of these suffered from severe depression over his studies. He came to rely on Margaret, Eddie and John, whose understanding and acceptance were an important element in his gradual recovery and success in obtaining a degree and founding a family.

Discussing a visitor, Eddie once remarked to Brendan, 'It's a pity X doesn't realize that you don't solve problems, you love them.'

'When I thought what this meant for Edward himself, I could see how much he shared with others what he had first lived through. Perhaps this was why people with disabilities felt so helped by him – simply because his own physical handicap could not be "solved". By loving, Eddie had actually left his handicap behind.

'This gave him the art of so focusing on other people's problems as to forget his own. He once wrote a poem, "Courage on a bicycle" which revealed his understanding of a young friend whose handicap caused him difficulties riding a bike. This sensitive lad was delighted to be given this poem after Eddie's death. It recalled Eddie's complete love for him, which, forgetting himself, could appreciate his handicapped friend's courage in mounting and riding a bicycle. He remembered how, with Eddie, he had never felt criticized or threatened, as he might have done by someone successful.'

Courage on a Bicycle

I see courage riding a bike
Holding both hands firm,
Steering a path of hope.
He has the guts
Of childhood questioning innocence.
Though dedicated to his own goal
He fights all for justice,
Justice as he sees it,
The playful and individual spirits
Of all that his age partakes.

Sometimes courage rolls through
All that gets in his way;
But that is the proof
Of his truth towards the world and himself.
No Obstacles shall ever overcome
This tyrant of his own ends,
Not the cruel despot who suppresses others,

He is only the surveyor of all
That he possesses within himself,
The animal inside that feeds on potential.

Courage always stands up to the fight
And moves awkwardly but surely forward.
He leads his battalion in meaningful encounters
Through the treadmill of heartbreak leading to
    manhood.
This tremendous urge that never listens
To other people's advice
That describe their versions of practical reality.
He storms after, grasps and embraces
Everything that he has seen and everything he
    has fallen on
Till reality belongs to him and advises his heart
    and his soul.

Margaret has a hilarious memory of her son's concrete advice to a close friend who was undecided whether to become a Focolarino or not. Pádraic Smyth had been invited to a Gen Congress in Rome. He was working in a hotel miles from Killarney. Since there was no bus to get to the station, his only hope to catch the appropriate train was to thumb a lift. He rang Eddie to tell him he saw no hope of getting to Rome, since no car would stop for him. Eddie replied, 'Pádraic, I believe God wants you to go to Rome. Get back on the road. My mother and I will be in unity with you praying for a car to stop.' A quarter of an hour later, the phone rang again. It was Pádraic asking Eddie to ring round Dublin to try and find a substitute to use his air ticket, since no car would stop. 'Pádraic, keep calm and just get back on that road.' Eddie, of course, knew that his small hotel salary made a taxi out of the question. As soon as he put the phone down, he rang his friend, Father Ronan, to beg him to meet Pádraic's train and rush him to the airport. A series of impossibilities followed. An Irish train was ten minutes early! Ronan had never met Pádraic. Was he even on the train? Eventually, an unexpected intuition showed him the right man. He hurried Pádraic to the car, feeling they were bound to be too late. Imagine their astonishment to find the plane was fifteen minutes late on its way to London!

Perhaps Brendan Purcell has given most thought to the secret of Eddie's relationship with other people. Brendan was mesmerized by his constant joy which seemed to spring from his humility as someone who was 'almost pure relation, pure receptivity that was also a gift . . . I think you could say that his happiness flowed from his being really an icon (rather a large one) of the life of the Trinity. Not that Eddie would have wanted to put it like that. But I wonder if that wasn't the secret of his utter openness – his being the kind of person no one ever felt suffocated by, threatened by, and therefore was happy to relate to.

'I can't recall Eddie speaking disparagingly of anyone. Nor did he ever seem to need to be noticed, say at a meeting or a Mariapolis. This didn't mean that nothing mattered to him. Ed would really suffer when it came home to him that he could not take part in an event he had been looking forward to, like a Gen Congress in Rome. Then he'd dig deeper, lose once again and find the key to another door that seemed closed, and often write a new song about his experience.'

Brendan came to realize that a great part of Eddie's gift to him was his special love for the 'Word of Life', the Focolare practice of taking a verse of Scripture lived out month by month. This love was expressed in the song, 'The Word' to which Marian contributed the music after her return from that vital Congress in Rome which produced in her the change for which Eddie had waited so long. This inspired the second verse.

The Word

The Word, Jesus, God the Son, made man,
Concealed, working inside your life,
Treasuring, treasuring the life within. (x2)

I've changed, can't you see it in my face,
Rearranged, left old ways without a trace.
Thank you, for giving me new life. (x2)

Refrain: I see it's true, I know it's true.
Yes, I can go ahead with You.

I can't fully understand, yet I feel I know His
Love.
We've become 'one' and 'I' has turned to 'we'.
All has come through His Word lived.

His intense living of the monthly Word had given him a deep insight into the presence of Jesus Forsaken and suffering in every person he met, to the point where, as Brendan remarked, 'He exhibited the fact that to love Jesus Forsaken really worked; that you don't have to worry so much about doing things or being important. He upturned any notions I might have had about what was needed to build a Christian community. By being there to love, all the time, even if it cost him a lot, that's all that was needed, and if you knew Eddie, you saw it working.'

His family 'saw it working' in the growing number of people with problems who became Eddie's friends. What might be called his clientele on the margins of society became enormous. Most of these have moved

86

on, but we are deeply indebted to one of them whom we shall call Kevin and who has generously sent us a detailed account of his adventures, so that he can speak from first hand experience for all the others.

'I first met Eddie through Paul O'Hara, an old school pal of mine. Paul was very good at maths and went on to college.

'My background was very disturbed. My father was a violent alcoholic. I had serious emotional problems. Also, I was a bit of a rebel at school, and failed my Leaving Certificate. Physically I was unwell too – I had a kidney removed when I was eighteen.

'Four to six years after leaving school, I bumped into Paul O'Hara again. We had gone our separate ways. At this stage I had become a seasoned alcoholic (whisky, beer), pillpopper (30 mgs valium a day) and my sexual relationships were with prostitutes. I was a crazy mixed-up kid!

'Anyway, I bumped into Paul. I admired him. I listened to him; I knew him. He had achieved a masters degree in maths. He was exuberant, enthusiastic. I was dead. He was really glad to see me – he seemed genuinely interested in me. He shared with me how he hadn't achieved the grades he wanted and how he fell in love with some girl but lost her. These things had shattered him. He told me how he had met Brendan Purcell and how he was now on the right road again. He wanted me to meet Eddie. I was overcome by his genuine concern for me.

'Who was this Eddie anyhow? You see, I was drunk when I met Paul. He just insisted that I meet Eddie, Margaret and John. Paul came into the pub with me. I got a top up. He had one "to be in unity with me", and then we walked miles to Eddie's house in Rathfarnham.

'I don't recall much, if anything, of my first encounter other than anti-climax. "Is this it?" I asked myself. But

Eddie was to haunt me for years to come. My drinking had progressed and many of my experiences at that time were "black-outs" – I don't remember events. In spite of that, I do recall:

'(1) Eddie had kind, sad, piercing eyes.

'(2) He communicated softly through his eyes.

'(3) His difficulty in speech (Eddie had a slight stutter) complemented his enormous "effort" to love. You could feel from the bottom of your gut the difficulty, struggle, he made to communicate; to reach out to me: to let me know that I too am important. His movements (he was in a wheelchair) were very restricted. I, too, was handicapped – but was locked into mine – lost. Eddie had overcome his. Me – I couldn't feel; give – I was like a zombie but also I was like a volcano ready to erupt.

'In Eddie the spirit (flame) in him was alive (burning). His body was his cage. In me, the spirit was dead. Eddie, Paul, Margaret – were going to rekindle it.

'All these things were a crossroads in my life . . . "I parched that dawn might yet appear and lead the way to light eternity." Eddie told me how he had tried to get into college and had failed – this I could identify with. I had no physical disability yet I was pathetic beside Eddie.

'(4) At some meeting (it may have been the first) Eddie asked me to bring him to the toilet. There were others there too, but he asked me. I pushed him down the hall and into the bathroom. Now toileting Eddie meant literally doing everything for him. I wouldn't let anybody toilet me – I'd be too embarrassed – I wouldn't let anybody get that close to me. But Eddie did and

I was shocked, awed, privileged. Years later I toileted my grandfather when he was dying. Also I worked as an attendant at a hospice for the dying and was privileged to "serve" in love and joy. Eddie had inspired me.

'Next, I found myself in a detox unit, which Eddie and Paul encouraged me to join. I came out of there well, but then had a very big row at home and went on a massive binge. I ended up in a psychiatric hospital. I was put on panaldehyde there and it was great. I manipulated all my fellow-patients to give me their medication, which they did, and I was in a continual buzz. One of the cleaning girls robbed medication out of the pharmacy for me and I ended up in a terrible fever with spots all over my body. Anyway, I had to be separated from the rest of the ward. I was locked up for ten days in a room and the sisters told me I was certified and that I could be locked up forever or put in a straitjacket. It was in this room that I first asked God to help me. I was delirious, demented, hallucinating, my stomach was locked in a knot – I was broken. My mother was allowed to say "Hello" to me at the door, but she just stood there and the tears fell out of her eyes. She said nothing. I told this to the shrink next day. He said, "You're responsible." I was alone. I was talking to myself. I looked for some way to swish through the window or something sharp to hurt myself with. I thought – somebody must be able to help me – why not ask God? I thought, "Yes, why not?" Then I said in all humility, "Dear God, please help me!" As soon as I did this my stomach began to unlock. I couldn't believe it. I cried. Always in the background was the direction and guidance from Paul and Eddie. Anyway, my skin everywhere on my body began to peel (like a metamorphosis). I remember hiding my hands in "group" because of my skin peeling. Eventually my time came to be let out of my room. It was like I had been in jail forever. The next day I was allowed into group therapy with a Father Raphael Short. Here I was put through the "wringer" as they say – "The truth shall set you free – but first it will make you miserable."

'I used to dash from the group to the phone to ring Eddie. Always he consoled and reassured me. He reminded me that I wasn't a bad person trying to get good but a broken person trying to get whole. Paul had sent letters and cards thanking me for showing him Jesus Forsaken. I just didn't understand all this love and attention. I got great help from "My night has no darkness" (which Paul sent me), and used to read it again and again walking up and down the hospital garden. I was introduced to Alcoholics Anonymous in the hospital too, and their spiritual programme of recovery. I felt at home among sinners. Later I could see how A.A. was like a candy store for a kid who wanted to help others. There were so many people who could be helped the way I was.

'But could I ever thank Eddie and Paul and Margaret and John for all their help? Because they were all in it together – in unity. I can only say that I have tried to love the way they taught me. In a way I believe that Eddie lives through me in my response to others in need.

'When I came out of hospital I was still very confused and frightened. I felt ashamed and avoided calling up Eddie. I saw myself, what I had become and felt unworthy beside someone so good and pure as he was. Eddie loved me as I was, but I couldn't. I had a long way to go yet. He wrote (now he could hardly move at all) a letter to me, asking me to give him a shout. I did, but I was very uneasy in myself. It was like I was in a limbo. Even as I write, I can feel Eddie's tender nature touching me. I feel like one of the lepers that Jesus healed but didn't return to thank him. I know, of course, that I must have thanked Eddie but I had a lot to learn. You see, my life turned completely about as a result of these encounters and always Eddie was in the background as a support and model.'

Eddie's letter which provoked his friend's reactions, one of the few to survive, illustrates his tender concern for each person who sought his help, as though he or she was the only one in the world who mattered to him at the moment of writing.

4 August '77.
SUMMER IS HERE !

Dear Kevin,

I will not start off by saying how are you? because Paul told me he saw you last week and and said you were well. Now that I know how you are [out of hospital], I want to hear of your state of well being myself. So, Kevin, I would be really delighted to see or hear from you very soon!!

I'll close now, Kevin, saving all the news until we can speak to each other directly. And if you feel awkward or embarrassed, *don't*! because such things should not exist amongst friends.

Waiting for you, Kevin,
Eddie.

To understand something of what Kevin found lived out in Eddie, it is perhaps useful to look at the meditation by Chiara that Kevin found so helpful:

My Night Has No Darkness

. . .Talking to the Focolarini, I spoke to them about a phrase. It was this: 'Jesus forsaken, embraced, pressed to ourselves, consumed in one with us, we consumed in one with him, made into suffering with him suffering, this is how we become (by participation) God, Love.'

This phrase struck me particularly. With the Focolarini we agreed to live well that Jesus forsaken 'pressed to ourselves, consumed in one with us, we consumed in one with him', where there is no longer, so to speak, I and Jesus forsaken, but we are one: 'made into suffering with him suffering, this is how to become Love, God.' I liked 'almost there not being two of us': I and Jesus forsaken, that is to say, I and the suffering that comes, I and the suffering that comes to me, I and my discovering it and then bit by bit embracing it and taking some seconds ... no, it must at once connect. Made suffering, with him suffering, only to want that, this is how to become God, Love.

Father Mario Strada sent me some photographs of the very beautiful frescos of his little church. Beneath one fresco there is this phrase: 'Nox mea obscurum non habet' (my night has no darkness). I liked this very much. It was as though it had been the Lord who had sent it because I thought: 'this is what I want to live' that is I must embrace suffering the moment it comes, straightaway, I must press it to myself as I do with the Eucharist, consume it in one with me, I consumed in one with him, made suffering with him suffering, this is how to become not suffering but Love, God.

For a few days now I have been concentrating on this and I have seen that it is the summary of all the Ideal, because Jesus forsaken is the Word of God fully expressed, open, therefore if you live Jesus forsaken, you live all the Gospel. Then I nourish myself with this word because I consume him in me and he consumes me in him . . . I have seen that living the whole day like this, this is an astounding tonic for the soul. When you begin your morning perhaps you feel a little tiredness: this is great 'my night has no darkness', that is to say this suffering does not exist because I love it. If they pose me difficulties, problems, within me I think: this is great, Jesus, here we are, look I embrace you, I press you to myself, myself made suffering with you. . . 'my night has no darkness'. Then forward the same way all day. I believe that spiritually you progress more in a week living this one thing, than you would in months and months living in another way.

Brendan recalled Kevin's story after Eddie had died. 'Some years later, while giving an evening class in psychology at University College, Dublin – about 1981 or so, one of the students – who were all adults who worked during the day – came up to me and introduced himself as Kevin. I was amazed, as I hadn't seen him for some years. He had, by that time, got himself a job and had also got married. He and his wife now had three lovely children.'

10

The Race towards God

Eddie's life was gathering such momentum that he must have found it difficult to cope with a rapid succession of events, involving him in the most varied ways.

During the previous year, he had become linked with three other young men confined to wheelchairs: Wolfgang in Austria who suffered from muscular dystrophy like himself, Imandar, a Sicilian, and Pepe Porquedou, an Italian, both road-crash victims. In a close correspondence, he had shared with them Chiara's insight into the role of those who suffer:

'It is not necessary to see the fruits. For example, I am convinced that those who bear most fruits are sometimes the most hidden ones, like the elderly whose goodness is known only to God, or sisters in enclosed convents, or those who suffer. The Holy Father himself says he has most confidence in those who suffer, because *they are like the roots of the tree* and so the cause of the fruits. Therefore, it is not necessary to see the fruits. It is necessary to be in the will of God, so that we remain in him and he remains in us. Then, certainly, we will bear many fruits.'

This meditation moved Eddie to write to Chiara at the beginning of 1976 to suggest that those 'in the world of suffering' should become a separate branch of the Focolare Movement. Half-way through his letter, he realized this was a contradiction 'because we always have the cross – we are already the roots of the tree'!

He then mentions a problem we know to have caused him and his mother grave difficulties. So weak were his muscles that the slightest cold filled his lungs with immovable phlegm requiring drastic action to dislodge it.

'Recently I spent two days in bed with a cold which prevented me going to a community meeting, which was a suffering. Remembering what you said, "with Jesus in the midst there is no distance", I remained in unity with everyone. As I felt better during my second day in bed, many Gen phoned me and I spoke to them from my bed. I was so happy because I had experienced exactly what you had said. Being ill and confined to bed could not prevent Jesus in the midst. This experience struck me very forcibly, how we in the "world of suffering" can experience at the *deepest level everything* you share at the various conferences. In a sense we are a testing ground where everything can be lived at the *strongest* level of love – Jesus Forsaken . . . "With Jesus in the midst there is no distance". That is enough. By *living* that, I can *understand* the whole *reality* of what you have talked about!

'Chiara, it is very difficult to express . . . what is deep within my heart and soul . . . but Jesus, the person, is amongst us and he will explain everything! So we will remain united and see what a wonderful *plan* God has *designed* for those of us who are – smiling – suffering!

'Certain that Jesus is among us!

Your *Radix*.'

Little did he expect the next move in God's plan. Almost immediately, he found himself transported to Rome in the company of David Hickey, taking part in a Gen Congress with hundreds of young men from many nations. Chiara staggered them all with her powerful conferences on 'Jesus in the Eucharist'.

It was a revelation to Eddie that the Eucharist unites us so closely to Christ that we become living Eucharists, other Christs, made one with each other by the Sacrament itself. He was deeply impressed by Pope Paul VI's confirmation of this which Chiara quoted:

'Pope Paul VI, uses incomparable expressions to describe the Eucharist. I shall quote just one of them: "...the Eucharist ... was instituted to make us brothers ..., so that from being strangers who are scattered apart and indifferent towards one another, we become united, equals and friends. It is given to us so that from being an apathetic, egoistic mass, from people divided and hostile to one another, we become a people, a true people, believing and loving, one heart and one soul." '

Chiara commented that in the Focolare everyone tried to live the reality of Pope Paul's vision: 'Our Ideal is the Ideal of unity. Do you not think it indicative that when Jesus addressed his Father in that famous prayer, he asked for unity among his followers and among those who would come after him, *after* he had instituted the Eucharist which made such a thing possible? Jesus, leaving the house on his way to the Garden of Olives, prayed, "Holy Father, keep them in your name which you have given me, that they may be one, even as we are one" (John 17:11).

'Through the Eucharist we are one with each other as the Father and the Son are one.

' "I do not pray for these only, but also for those who are to believe in me through their word, that they may all be one, even as you, Father, are in me, and I in you, that they also may be in us, so that the world may believe that you have sent me" (John 17:20-21).

'But we are in Jesus who is in the Father, through the Eucharist.

' "The glory which you have given me I have given to them, that they may be one even as we are one, I in them and you in me, that they may become perfectly one . . ." (John 17:22-23).

'We cannot enter the kingdom except in unity with Jesus and with one another through the Eucharist, a unity which is like that of the Father and the Son who are one!

'Therefore, if we love our great Ideal, our vocation to unity, we must love the Eucharist passionately.'

No wonder Eddie wrote to Chiara:

Congresso Gen, '76

Dearest Chiara,

Thank you for your message which we received today at the Congress. It was beautiful; with your promise to keep Jesus in the midst, I can leave the Congress tomorrow with a great hope and a great joy.

Now I promise to keep Jesus in the midst with you and so we can make the joy of Jesus complete.

One in Mary.

Radix.

PS As you will gather from this letter I really did reach the Congress!

RADIX FROM DUBLIN

In this letter, Eddie shows that at the Gen Congress he must have caught an echo of the meditation he knew so well, an echo which links the Eucharist and his vocation to be like another Mary.

I went into church one day,
and with my heart full of trust, I asked:
'Why did you wish to remain on earth,
on every point of the earth,
in the most sweet Eucharist,
and you have not found
– you who are God –
also a way to bring and to leave here
Mary, the mother of all of us who journey?'
In the silence he seemed to reply:
'I have not left her because I want to see her again
        in you.
Even if you are not immaculate,
my love will virginize you,
and you, all of you,
will open your arms and hearts as mothers of
        humanity,
which, as in times past, thirsts for God
and for his mother.
It is you who now
must soothe pains, soothe wounds
dry tears.
Sing her litanies
and strive to mirror yourself in them.'

(*Meditations*, New City, London, 1989 p.52f.)

1976 was proving to be the happiest period Eddie
had experienced since he had come to know Chiara.
His culminating joy came in the June of that year
when Bruno Carrera arrived in Dublin to fulfil Chiara's
prediction of three years before and open the Men's
Focolare in the flat Eddie and his friends had been
preparing since the last days of 1975.

Eddie had written to Chiara an urgent appeal in 1973:

'Recently, many boys and seminarians have come to know the Ideal of unity. They are very loving boys and hungry to know more. The three Focolarine, Pina, Mary and Lieta, love us very much and for this we are very happy. But it is not possible for them to help everybody, as it would be if there was a Men's Focolare here. Then many good boys would come to know the Ideal. In Ireland there are very many good boys searching for something that will last and in the Ideal we have the answer for them.

'I do not wish to worry you with this. We are glad to keep on living and this is important, but the grace we would receive from a Men's Focolare would be beautiful.

'Thank you, Chiara, for what you have given us and you can be assured of all our unity and love.'

Chiara had replied that same year.

'Dear Eddie and Friends,

I was very happy to receive your letter . . . Though it is not possible to open a Men's Focolare in Ireland at this time, God willing, the moment will come. In the meantime, you can prepare the ground by setting "mines" of love and keeping the flame of Jesus in your midst constantly burning. This is my wish for you and I entrust you all to Mary.

In her, *Chiara*.'

From a report that Eddie wrote, we can see how busy the Gen had been setting those 'mines'*. Now, at last, Eddie's cup was full, with his long cherished dream on the point of fulfilment.

At the same time for a whole year Eddie pondered deeply

---

* See pp. 109-112.

on all he had heard in Rome, asking what it meant for him personally. It was then that he wrote his last letter to Chiara. He was still haunted by his longing to become a Focolarino. Prompted by a great event, Italy's National Eucharistic Congress in which Chiara was deeply involved, he wrote to share his longing.

Dublin, 1977.

Dearest Mother,

I write to share my heart and soul with you and I do this with perfect trust like a baby with his mother.

Lately, I spoke with Dimitri, our capozona*, and I asked him how I could become a Focolarino, being physically handicapped. He told me that, in point of fact, from the juridical point of view, it was not possible for me or anyone in my position to become a Focolarino. This was a great sadness for me. Dimitri went on to show me how this situation gave me the possibility of living the Ideal in its purest form, since the true test of a Focolarino comes when he is deprived of all structures. He said many other things, but that phrase struck me most forcibly.

So, Chiara, after that conversation, I feel a strong desire to consecrate myself immediately to God. I cannot manage to say much more, except that every day I experience my helplessness and my nothingness, as I am slowly being formed in my vocation, that of being Mary. So, now, in unity with you, Chiara, I wait to see what direction my life must take, since I will only be able to discover God's will for me in unity with you.

---

* Capozona: the person in charge of the Zone of Britain and Ireland for the Movement.

Meanwhile, as I await your reply, I shall continue to live in my Gen unit, being Jesus Eucharist for each person.

Ciao, Chiara. I offer everything for the Eucharistic Congress,

Your *Radix*.

Chiara replied by the end of the year.

Rocca di Papa, 26/10/77.

Dearest Radix,

I want to thank you specially for having opened your soul to me. I rejoice with you over all that Jesus is bringing to birth within you, for his gaze of love on you, for the call you feel to give your life to him.

With regard to the manner of realizing this, I am of the same opinion as Dimitri and I am happy that you continue to examine everything in unity with him.

Ciao, Radix! I greet you from my heart, desiring your holiness. In the race towards God,

Chiara.

Bruno's arrival gave a new dimension to his life. His home was no longer the meeting place of his friends, a sacrifice he gladly made, as John took him twice a week to the Focolare in Dundrum. Bruno always needed him there. Their friendship led him to think of Eddie as a member of his small community. He recalled:

'His presence was so important, as a friend and to keep Jesus in the midst. He was someone who was really part of the family, he wanted to live in the Focolare and to be a Focolarino, but this wasn't possible. Yet at heart he was much more a Focolarino than anything else. I remember the special love he had for Mary. Mary was always silent, couldn't do anything in a sense, yet living only for Jesus.

'You could experience it. His wisdom and his unity were stronger than anyone else's, as he sat there grasping everything, his face shining. Personally, I felt extremely close to him, even closer than to the Focolarini in the Focolare; he was always the first one I brought up to date with news.

'He made himself one with each person he met to an extraordinary degree and was everything that Chiara desired. His sense of peace and happiness radiated from him and he continually transmitted it to the others. He was always so full of joy and never complained.

'His sense of apostolate was very strong too. He kept in continual contact with those he was cultivating in the life of the Gospel. He never once forgot anyone and I think everyone always felt at home with him.'

Eddie's life continued to make an impact on a wide circle of other people. He was always a rock of encouragement. Following the Mariapolis in 1977, a young Kerryman at that time studying to be a Jesuit, whom we shall call Eamonn, began to keep in touch with Eddie who had made a deep impression on him. The Mariapolis was a turning point in his life; a force which propelled him out of himself towards other people. The Eucharist began to mean so much more to him, and he felt that the Mariapolis was a foretaste of Heaven. Yet he was in a state of confusion. It was Eddie to whom he confided his chaotic inner struggle.

'In October 1977 I went to Milltown Park, the Jesuit House of Studies, to study. After a month there, I discovered that this was a very beautiful vocation, but not for me. I went to Eddie to tell him, and he was a strong support. I was feeling dreadfully insecure and full of doubts. I just wanted to speak to him because he was as solid as a rock.

'I felt so like nothing beside him; my problems paled into nothingness beside his. I was deeply impressed by his life which was so deep and his love which was so relaxed. I felt deeply drawn to him. He was very ordinary, yet very special. You see he was always so understanding and I knew I could count on him and ring him at any time.

'I had been suffering with an ulcer and in March, 1978, I finally made up my mind to leave the Jesuits. I had been close to an old priest who lived in Rathfarnham Castle and I was afraid to tell him of my decision. I thought he would be hurt. I went to see Eddie who encouraged me to tell him. I had built up a good relationship with this old priest and with several students I played cards with. Through this old priest and Eddie, they gradually found themselves in the Movement too. The priest wished me well, gave me a book and told me he understood.

'I remember well the 14th March, 1978. It was a windy, desolate sort of day and I had driven to a grim, basement flat in Howth where I was to stay with my sister. She didn't turn up for the weekend and I was entirely alone and in a state of desolation, very unsure of myself and of where I was heading. It was then that I rang Eddie. I felt he understood straight away. I used to ring him every day and he helped me to try and love Jesus Forsaken.

'Everything I had wanted was taken away from me. I felt completely blocked – I was no longer on the road to being a priest, a Jesuit, and nothing in the world attracted me. Eddie helped me to love and accept Jesus in those moments as the Forsaken One. Through Eddie's love and unity I got to know him better. I was so ashamed of myself and always felt that Eddie was pure compassion.

'After a while I got a job as a remedial teacher in a very tough school. Now I had no time to worry about myself; I was always so tired and used to come home from school so exhausted that I went straight to bed.

'Eddie used to ring me and when I was down, which

was frequently, he would lift me and bring me back to Jesus as the centre of my life. Many men, when they leave religious life, give up everything, but I didn't know what to do. Should I go to daily Communion? Seeing Eddie and the other Gen doing this made me want to as well. I made a decision then that this was the life I wanted to lead for the rest of my life.

'Gradually, through Eddie's nurturing, I was drawn to the Focolare and the other Gen and pretty quickly I found myself in a Gen unit.'

Then Eamonn's conquest of himself began in earnest. At the Mariapolis in 1979 he remembers sleeping in the same room as Eddie for one night, and he was delighted to get the opportunity. He fell asleep full of enthusiasm to help him, but about 3 o'clock Eddie called out that he needed to be turned.

'I was annoyed and really had to overcome this, as I was very attached to my sleep and comfort. This happened twice throughout the night. Now, I really treasure that experience.'

Later he realized that this was the measure. He had to die, i.e., lose his immediate desires in order to allow Jesus to enter his relationship with every person he met. This was revealed to him by a play. The Gen had taken Eddie to see 'Waiting for Godot'. Afterwards, Eddie expressed some views, and Eamonn reacted angrily against them.

'I was very attached to my own ideas about the play and about Beckett. Eddie turned to me and said:

"Eamonn, I don't feel we have Jesus in the midst."

'I knew it was true, but I was angry. I thought, do I even have to lose this? I've lost the Jesuits, being a priest, do I now have to lose my own ideas as well?'

But it was precisely in that losing that, together with Eddie, he began to live a new life.

Another young man who had just left university to start a wholesale fish business in Skerries, North Dublin, came to the Mariapolis.

'There I was very impressed by Bruno, and though I had never met him before, he seemed very interested in what I was doing. It was a genuine interest and not just a question of making conversation.

'I was also very struck by Eddie. He asked me to push him in his wheelchair; it was a trick he had for getting to know people. Then he asked me to feed him. Somehow you never felt you were being charitable towards him; he seemed to use his handicap to love and draw you out. I had a very "come day go day" attitude to the Movement.

'I had started up this fish business and at the beginning it was going reasonably well; then it started to cave in. I couldn't sleep at night with worry. Throughout the day I felt nauseous and faint. I had been going over to Eddie's religiously every Sunday, but during this shaky period I would phone regularly telling him my problems. It was like a call to the Samaritans. He really helped me over the hump until the business got on its feet again.

'I was now in a Gen unit, although Ed never pushed me. He would always say I should go to Bruno, I should go to the Focolare and I said "Yes" and kept going to Eddie's. Eddie used to call me a "chancer".

'Afterwards I understood that the source of the charism of unity was the Focolare and life finally sorted itself out. Eddie came to Skerries a few times and met my parents. He was a very special sort of person and my parents really loved him; they were unaware of his handicap. Eddie was like a black hole in space. Able to absorb people and their worries and problems. Funnily enough, he never seemed to have too many himself.

'I remember when Chiara received the Templeton Prize

for Progress in Religion,* I really wouldn't have gone, only Eddie asked me to. I went on a plane with him and sat up front really getting V.I.P. treatment. That was a very special time.

'I remember too that Eddie had to use the bathroom and, as I had never assisted anyone before, I really dreaded it. But Eddie had asked me to help him. It must have been embarrassing and humiliating for him, yet he made the situation light and it was an opportunity for me to do something for him.'

Many priests, also, were helped by Eddie. They felt he was a light and showed them how to build up their communities. Brendan Purcell remembers this aspect of his influence, recalling his saying, 'You shouldn't drop the Word, the way you wouldn't drop the Eucharist', and how he lived the Word of Life consistently in the nitty gritty of each day.

'He was a most revolutionary person. I saw him change people; they became builders of community. The paradox of his life was that instead of doing things, he was directing a source of renewal, as someone who built up communion. He really lived "the new civilization of love" and was the most radical revolutionary I knew – a real priest from the Royal Priesthood, changing himself and changing those around him. He always loved with the purity of God because he loved everyone without self-interest, and because of this detachment, he made profound unity with anyone he met. Because of this purity and self-control in his relationships with people, his love was for them and not for himself.'

Brendan felt this in the warmth of the Gen Masses in Eddie's home on Sundays, 'There was a tremendous

---

* In 1977. The prize-giving was in the Guildhall, London.

transparence of a group who were trying to share everything, both spiritually and practically. Eddie was there, a living Jesus Forsaken, always smiling.'

Pat Delaney put it like this:

'There was Eddie's pivotal role in our Gen unit. Our unit was composed of quite diverse personalities, and he was a living example of the weakest, a great binding force who always wanted to keep Jesus among us.

'When the Focolare came to Dublin, Eddie received it with great joy. At the same time, it was also a further period of losing for him, as things ceased to be the way they were before. The activities of the boys no longer revolved around the bungalow in Rathfarnham but were now centred on the Focolare, which is precisely what Eddie wanted but at the same time, he had to lose out on being the centre of activity. He was an inspiration to us of how to lose our attachments well. He never made his suffering obvious.

'Eddie would always try to bring unity to the group, sorting out the difficulties and acting as a catalyst.

'At the beginning, when I first met him, Eddie was very conscious of himself as a man. This was something which caused him less pain as he grew spiritually; in fact, I would say that as he grew weaker physically he grew stronger spiritually.'

Chiara was constantly originating new ways for the Gen to live the Gospel. In 1978 she gave them the idea of going to 'Die for your own people'.

'The Gen aren't complete if they don't root themselves in their own country. And something that a Focolarino said comes to my mind. He was just leaving the centre of the Movement where he had been formed, to go back to his own country which was far away and full of dangers.

' "We'll meet again, perhaps in heaven. Let me have all the news of the Movement," and then he added, knowing he would not return, "I'm going ready to die for my own people."

'This is what each of us has to feel: that we have "to die for our own people". Some of you might ask me: but who are our people? There are no poor in our country . . . Look around, Gen, aren't there young people everywhere who have been cut off: marginalized, drug addicts, atheists? There's no place on earth where there aren't people like these. And they are our own people.

'You asked me about something else as well: "What about the openness towards other religions which you talked about, how can we have this same dimension now?"

'Don't you see that this openness also includes those without God? In fact, at the end of my speech at the Guildhall in London [at the giving of the Templeton Prize], I talked among other things about the "poorest of the poor, poor because they don't have God". This sentence struck a lot of people, so much so that there were two English journalists who used it as the heading for the article they were doing on the Templeton Prize: "The poorest of the poor", as if I worked for a Movement specifically for atheists; and they had been really impressed by "those who most pain our hearts".

'And so we need to find our local "Jesus Forsaken" so as to "die for our own people".'

In the summer of 1976, the World Gen Centre in Rome had sent their representative, Peppuccio, to visit the Gen in Dublin. Eddie and his friends worked strenuously to prepare a flat for him. His visit made a powerful impression and it was followed up with a visit from Turi, another member of the Rome team. He brought with him Chiara's latest thoughts on 'dying for your own people', which evoked a deep echo in Eddie's heart. Soon after his visit, Eddie sent this detailed report to Peppuccio:

'Greetings from all the Gen in Ireland. Turi's visit was very special because he gave us a new understanding of what being a Gen means. He also brought us the world dimension of the Gen. We learnt so many things during the two days we spent with him. He prepared us to take a new step forward as Gen. At the end of his visit we felt very happy because we had really got to know him and he us very quickly. Because of this we found a new strength and commitment to the life of unity.'

By this time, the group of Gen Eddie met with, his original unit, had grown so much as to have been made into two units.

'The effects from the graces we received can best be measured by the life in our two units since his visit. To give you a better picture we will deal with each separately.

'First of all, Unit A – for which Gerard Mulligan is responsible. In this unit we have become more aware of what being a Gen unit means and gradually a greater commitment has grown. As we have got to know each other better, the relationships between us have become more like those in a family. We have become very much more open to one another. This has become more evident when trying to see what prayer and "Dying for your own people" mean for us. As we pondered these points together we soon discovered that we all had our own ideas, which differed greatly. But we have come to realize that it is for unity that we meet together and not to hold on to our own ideas or to discuss our own particular problems.

'We have not yet seen exactly what "Dying for your own people" means for us concretely, but we have realized that we have to reach the point of dying for one another first.

'Also we have realized the importance of keeping in touch with one another, so we are now making bigger efforts to keep in close contact. During Christmas we could not see much of each other, because many of us had to leave Dublin to spend Christmas with our families. However, now that Christmas is over, we are back in regular contact again.

'Unit B – for which Brendan Gallagher is responsible. One of the first things we noticed was how different we all are in personality and also in the length of time we've been living as Gen. So, in the beginning, we had to be very patient with each other, especially those of us who had been Gen for a while, by not forcing on newcomers our idea of what being a Gen means. We had to leave them free. Now we have become sensitive to each other's needs, and the trust that this has built between us has made us very open to each other. At other times when we have not been united enough to have Jesus among us, we lacked this sensitivity; then we discovered how difficult and impossible things became.

'One of the main problems we have found is meeting each other outside our weekly meetings, because we live long distances from each other. But we are beginning to feel the need to be in closer contact by 'phone etc., and this is the most important thing. In fact, the one who lives the furthest away in a city on the other side of Ireland and who has the least contact, is the one with whom we feel the strongest unity.

'We usually have our unit meetings after supper together – a very good way to build unity. During the meetings we read some of the writings of Chiara, the commentary on the Word of Life and share experiences of applying it to life each day. Also we go through all the aspects of the spirituality to see how well we live each one. This is one of the best ways of deepening our unity.

'Two of the Gen, one from each unit, now share a flat together. Both units usually have their meetings in the flat, and so we help to support it mostly through the communion of goods and by keeping the place tidy, so that it reflects the life of a Christian.

'Just before Christmas, we had a party in the flat, and this went very well. Bruno and Eoin also came to it for a while. We bought and prepared food and drink together and it was all very simple; we talked, joked and really enjoyed ourselves. Parties with Jesus among us are really special.'

The months passed quickly and Eddie was getting weaker; he was already twenty-nine and had well passed the life-span that doctors had forecast for him. They had said that he would not live beyond his late teens, but God had had another plan and provided him with the years to fulfil it.

In October, 1979, at the bank holiday weekend, Eddie was able to join the Gen for their day-out in Avondale, Co. Wicklow. This proved to be his last trip with them. For the most part he sat in the car with someone beside him, while the others played football. It was a very special day, a day of real closeness, as though Eddie was aware that this was the last time they would relax together.

Early in November, he heard that his friend, Dori, had been involved in a car accident. Dori is Chiara's first companion in their adventure of unity. For some years, she had often visited Dublin to encourage the life springing up round Eddie. They exchanged many letters, but only one has survived, the one he wrote to her less than a month before he died. In parts, it is poignantly prophetic.

Dublin 5 November '79

Dear Dori,

I was very upset when I heard about your car accident and I hope by now you have fully recovered from it. Jesus Forsaken has certainly a most vivid imagination!

For me things are going very well, as the sense of unity becomes more and more a reality in my life. At times, it seems as if I understand even less than I did a few years ago – as if I had started to fall behind. But I am certain that is not true. It is just that these doubts are coming, so that I am not able even to have this consolation of unity in the Ideal anymore.

Recently, I was listening to a tape by Chiara ... I think she was talking to the Focolarini. Anyway, she was talking about the first times of the Movement and how all of you followed the will of God, and how he guided you. You died (spiritually) in a special way to be born in a special way. Whatever you first began, He destroyed and ruined, so that it became totally new and completely Him. This really struck me and the feeling came inside that I, too, was being destroyed and ruined through my physical disability to be born new and completely Him. This is what God wants from me and is asking of me in this particular way, just as he asks it of all of us but in different ways.

Everything now must be a preparation towards this. Already over the last few months, I've felt many times empty and completely nothing, and in this I have been very much in unity with Chiara. Yet I feel a great peace within me, knowing I have to do and have to be, nothing except completely Him. Because before I was preoccupied with what I *should* be doing.

During the last year, the Gen boys in Ireland have made a very strong experience, and this has come about especially from the life in the Gen units. They have reached a new maturity which can be seen in their lives with many new boys being drawn toward us. I am still with the Gen and we have about twenty Gen divided into four units, plus about ten pre-Gen. The visit of Pope John

Paul II and Gen Rosso was a real grace and has brought us into contact with many young people. Now we must work hard not to waste this grace.

I will stop writing now, Dori. All I wanted to do was to say hello, and share my life with you. You can always be sure of my unity and prayers, especially now you are weak.

United in Jesus Forsaken,
Radix.

Towards the end of November, Eddie had to go into hospital for X-rays. His health was deteriorating rapidly; there were sporadic shortages of oxygen to his brain which caused hallucinations and blackouts; he was finding it more and more difficult to support his head and he had many disturbing dreams. His illness was progressing to its conclusion.

The doctor who attended him, said it was a medical miracle that someone with such a severe form of muscular dystrophy should have outlived his teens. This doctor had studied the disease in the USA where it was quite the norm to have people with this form of the illness die at eighteen.

Eddie was a phenomenon – someone who had lived his life twice. The second time he lived it for God.

11

Mary, I Come Running to You

Pádraic Gilligan was so deeply shocked by Eddie's death that he immediately reacted in characteristic fashion. He recalls:

'I was nineteen when Eddie died. The main feature of my relationship with him was that he was always there. He was a focal point of tremendous consistency. I always felt that, no matter what I did, even if I were to go away from the Movement and not be interested in living the Gospel any more, my relationship with Eddie would have lasted because I felt he loved me for myself.

'I was the one who wrote Eddie's song which we still sing. It is sometimes called "To Mary" or just "Eddie's song". The verses were taken from a letter Eddie had written to Our Lady before he died. Margaret, his mother, passed this on to me. When he died I was desperately upset and this is one of the quickest pieces of music I have ever composed. I was in the back of David Hickey's car with Pat Delaney. In between the funeral home and my own home, I took the letter, wrote the verses and put them to music. I was really thrilled to have been able to do that as a tribute to Eddie and all he meant to me. Here it is.'

Eddie's Song

What can I say to you
When words only spoil everything
And your life speaks much louder than words
Because you are full of emptiness.

Why am I writing to you?
I don't know the reason
But every day brings me closer to you,
Closer to your nothingness.

You call out my name
And Mary, I come running to you,
Happy to be an open flower,
A sea of new creation.
Mary, I come running to you.

Mother, I am your child
Living in your silent way
And though I grow weaker now,
It makes me more like you each day.

Yours is the hidden way,
Chosen with a 'yes' so strong.
My secret 'yes' to you
Makes God my only vision now.

You call out my name
And Mary, I come running to you,
Happy to be an open flower,
A sea of new creation.
Mary, I come running to you.

Eddie's Mother can best tell us the story of his last hours in the letter she wrote to Chiara. After describing their life together before they learnt her story, Margaret continued:

'We both went through a period of quiet desperation. I was aware that if he did not find an answer to his problems at this stage, he would probably become an embittered person for the rest of his life. All day I would manage to keep cheerful, but at night in bed, the tears would flow, and I begged Our Lady to help me. I would say to her, "You suffered through your only Son and you can see how I am suffering through mine. Help me, please."

'It was during this period that we met the Ideal of unity. It was Mary's answer for us both. Tom Sherrard came to see us in Dublin and persuaded us to go to an ecumenical meeting near Rome. The theme of the meeting was "God is Love". We were enchanted with what we heard and inspired by what we understood. Radix was like a parched plant that had received water. We came back to Dublin and just longed to share our joy and experience with everyone but had understood that words were useless. Only our mutual love would bear witness and so a wonderful adventure began. Radix knew very few people in Dublin because we had only been living in Ireland for four years. He was mostly confined to the house, so it seemed impossible for him to reach out to others, but he prayed always to be made an instrument of his love, so that the Ideal would be known by many in Ireland. Little by little, people started coming to our house and we kept in close touch with the Focolare in London. They came over from time to time, and so a little plant of the Ideal was started here.

'Radix longed to see Loppiano and wrote to Dimitri who arranged for him to go. So we set off and spent two weeks there. For Radix it was the most wonderful experience of his life. On the evening before we came home, Maras told him, "Be like John and take Mary home to Ireland with you." Radix longed so much to be a Focolarino and spoke to Dimitri about it, although in his heart he knew this was something else he had to lose. After speaking with Dimitri he understood how the structures were not important. Only the choice of God was necessary and his role in the Ideal was different – it was just to "be", to "be" for all the others.

'As he grew weaker and weaker physically, he grew stronger spiritually. He helped such a variety of people. The Gen were always very close to him in a strong bond of unity. Through them many boys came to see him, those who were on drugs or were confused and on the point of breaking. To those who did not know the Ideal, it would seem strange that a poor, helpless boy in a wheelchair could help them. As he said himself, "All I can do is make myself one with them and listen, really listen." One of the nurses who came to help him, said the first time she met him, "He has such peace in him, I wish I knew his secret."

'The last few weeks he grew weaker and weaker and knew in his heart he would soon be going to God. On the 31st November he went to hospital for a chest X-ray and was asked to stay in for investigation. At first he protested, because he was worried that it would be difficult for the nurses to lift him, but when he realized there were male nurses on the ward, he readily agreed to stay.

'I pushed him in his wheelchair into the ward which, apart from one young man, was occupied by very old men. He looked around and said, "Now I know why I am here", because he could see they all looked lonely and in need of love. There was a crucifix on the wall behind him, so I whispered to him, "Your best friend is here too" and turned the chair for him to see. A big smile spread over his face, and he said, "Yes, Mum, my best friend always."

'One of the Gen who worked on the hospital catering staff, came hurrying to the ward as soon as he heard the news, hugged him and said. "Oh Radix, I always longed to have someone in this big hospital to share this presence of Jesus." That Sunday we were having a Focolare Community meeting and Radix insisted that I went. Other relations visited him in the afternoon. I went to the hospital straight from the meeting and suffered to see how weary and tired he looked. Another Volunteer* came in with me, and he told her, "Hospital is a beautiful place to be. Jesus Forsaken in so many people; so many to love."

'He wanted to know what had happened at the meeting, who had been there, what had been said and had Jesus been there. He was so concerned about the poor old man in the next bed – "It is a suffering. I cannot speak to him because he is deaf and I am unable to shout, but I smile when he looks at me. I hope he knows I love him, because he has no visitors." He made sure that any fruit brought into him was shared with Paddy. His father and I sat with him for another hour. Then he insisted we went home. Four times he said, "Go home and don't worry, I'm alright." I felt he was detaching himself from us.

'We came away with heavy hearts, hoping he would sleep well and feel better next day, but in the early hours of the morning his heart just stopped beating. The doctors did not realize that death was so near, but I am sure Radix did. He who had had to accept help from others to do the simplest things all his life, wanted this big step into eternity to be just between Jesus and himself.

---

* A member of the Volunteer branch of the Focolare Movement.

He had only been in hospital two-and-half days and yet the doctors and nurses wept openly as if they had suffered a personal loss. He looked so beautiful, Chiara, so beautiful.

'The Gen arranged his funeral Mass as he always wanted it, a celebration. Fourteen priests concelebrated Mass. The sun beamed through the stained glass windows of Mary and Joseph at the back of the altar. The Gen sang so beautifully and read your meditation, "I love you". They also sang a song to Mary, using the words of a letter Radix had written two days before he went into hospital. Father Brendan Purcell, a Focolarino priest, was the chief celebrant. He used to bring the Eucharist to Radix at home and hear his confession, and there was always a strong unity between them.

'Father Ronan Geary, a Jesuit priest who had known Radix many years, spoke from the pulpit. He said that everyone who first met Radix thought they would give him strength and comfort but always came away feeling they had received more than they had given. He also recalled how a few months before, Radix had felt very ill during the night and had said to me next morning, "If I ever die suddenly without being able to say goodbye to the Gen, give them my love, tell them to be faithful to the end and I will see them at the last banquet."

'Ronan explained that Radix has now entered God and each time we receive the Eucharist, we become God by participation, so are one with Radix. The church was packed to the doors with about 2,000 people. Those who did not know him, felt he must be someone important. In their amazement, they said, "We have never seen a funeral like this. It is more like a wedding." How true that was! Radix had gone to meet his Spouse. Many people said, "I will never fear death again after this morning."

'The Gen boys carried him to the grave and we sang "Maria" in farewell. He loved Mary so much and strove to imitate her nothingness. There was another funeral in the cemetery at the same time. The mourners thanked us and said how much our singing had helped them in their sorrow. I wish I could convey to you all that is in my heart, Chiara, but because you are my Mother, I know that you will understand. Thank you for giving us the Ideal which gave light to our Lives.

'Many friends. . . have asked me for a keepsake of Radix. It was only then that I realized that apart from his clothes, he owned nothing. Everything he had, he had given away. He died as he would have wanted, detached from everything except Jesus and Mary.

'All my love to you, Mama,
Margaret (Pearl).'

When Margaret had asked Chiara to give her a new name, she had simply translated 'Margaret' which in Latin means 'Pearl'; recalling the 'the pearl of great price' of the Gospel which a man having found, he will sell all that he has, to possess. This inbuilt Word of Life shines through Margaret's letter giving her the wisdom to understand and accept the manner of Eddie's passing.

Was it, perhaps, this same intuition that moved her to pass on Eddie's last letter to Pádraic Gilligan so soon after his death? She could scarcely have guessed that he would transform it into song with such speed, in time to be learnt and sung at her son's funeral for the consolation of all present and of hundreds ever since. Whatever the process of that happy inspiration, we must surely let Eddie have the last word that gave rise to it. This in itself is remarkable, since few people can have left this world with an explanation to Our Lady herself.

Dear Mary,

What can I say to you? Words seem only to spoil everything because your life speaks for itself. Why am I writing to you? I cannot answer even that. Maybe I write, yes I do write to you because I am helpless and each day I am getting a little bit more so. Not only can I not do anything but I feel I am becoming nothing. I know you are not surprised to receive this letter because who else could I write to about nothingness but the expert on nothingness yourself?

Now in the second paragraph — I am not sure it is right for the second paragraph — I will not make a mess of things by explaining you because how can you explain nothing? I want to tell you I am happy to be nothing because it gives me the opportunity to be a little like you, who in your lowliness chose the hidden way with a 'Yes' the world has never heard and will never hear again. What else could I be but happy with a chance to be part of this open flower, an immense sea of new creation?

Mother, I am your child and like you I am living in a silent way until all your children recognize you as their Mother.

May God be our only vision.

Radix.

EPITAPH

Settling Eddie down for the night was a constant problem for Margaret. She had to help him find a comfortable position. He used to tease her with his comment, 'I'm still in an uncomfortable position'. He suggested she should have his gravestone inscribed:

HERE LIES EDWARD McCAFFREY
STILL IN AN
UNCOMFORTABLE POSITION.

During his funeral Mass on that cold December morning, 1979, the congregation were mesmerized after the Gospel. A beautiful butterfly emerged from the flowers in front of the altar. It proceeded to fly over the book of the Gospels, over the heads of the fourteen concelebrants and on over the coffin, before finally disappearing into the rafters.

This was a symbol for Margaret and John and all their friends. At last Eddie was free of his chair.

He was no longer in an uncomfortable position!

On his gravestone in Mount Jerome Cemetery (Harold's Cross, Dublin) is written his word of life:

"But God chose what is foolish in the world to shame the wise" (1 Cor. 1:27).

ACKNOWLEDGEMENTS

No one would have thought of investigating Eddie McCaffrey's story, if Chiara Lubich and her companions had not been led by the Holy Spirit to the Ideal of Unity that lay hidden in the Gospel treasury awaiting the impulse of World War II. Eddie himself was the first to acknowledge his debt to her in a moving letter as early as 1971 (p. 40).

To Jean Byrne of Dublin we owe the essential research and basic structure of his book, whilst we are deeply indebted to his mother, Margaret Neylon, for the human details that make his story live. Eddie's friends in and beyond the Focolare Movement have been most generous in contributing their personal memories and treasured anecdotes.

To the Jordan family of my parish I am personally grateful for unstinting encouragement. To Kate who typed the manuscript, to Matthew who fed it into his computer and to Clare who reproduced several perfect copies, I can only say a heartfelt 'thank you.' Though none of them knew Eddie, they took him to their hearts as one of their own.

To all who are moved by Eddie's story, I would beg the favour of their prayers for the entire team whose countless members have made Eddie live again. Not least for those whose manuscripts have not actually been printed but whose insights have been vital to my grasp of Eddie's ordeal.

Maurus Green, O.S.B.